Pages of Poems by Paige

More of my poems about love, feelings and emotions, finding strength, healing, and uplifting inspiration

Author - Alisa Paige

1

Introduction

Find Your Passion Poem

It's hard to take the first step,
But my wanting for this I've always kept,
Way down, deep inside,
Where our hopes and dreams secretly hide,
I took a baby step and kept on going,
I get to share in my own way of showing,
And now finally I love what I do,
Find your passion and so will you.

Pages of Poems by Paige, poems to help flow through every aspect of life

Poetry Book Description

This is my second collection of over 100 heartfelt poems, and even more than in my first book "Poems by Paige", that I wrote to help bring calm, peace and love, to emotions that we all can relate to, and help with many types of feelings that we all deal with in life. Also, I hope to help inspire and uplift us all, as well as help to overcome many different obstacles we're given, which resonate within us all. I hope you enjoy them and that they touch you in some way. I love writing them, expressing myself and sharing them with the world. As always, peace and love and let things flow.

Book Dedication

This book is dedicated to my Kyle, my mom and dad, my husband, and to all my loved ones, family and friends. I'm so incredibly lucky to have you all and your support.
And as always, a special thank you to God!
Thank you all so much!
I love you all!

Chapter 1
<u>Love and Friendship</u>

Chapter 2
<u>Love and Loss</u>

Chapter 3
Emotions, Feelings and Coping

Chapter 4
Strength, Courage and Healing

Chapter 5
Inspirational and Uplifting

Chapter 1

Love and Friendship

Through My Rose Colored Glasses I See Poem

Through my rose colored glasses I see,
You are my sweet poetry,
You see me with sweet eyes,
To my sweet surprise,
I love you more than I knew,
I ever thought I could do,
Loving with no doubts,
You, I could never live without,
I didn't think that part,
Of me was a light, or a spark,
Of the love I feel for you,
And all along it grew,
And it grows to this day,
Whatever come, what may,
When I walk through the door,
I'll see your happiness I'm sure,
You're the happiness I seek,
When none, or part of me is weak,
You're always happy to be,
Around or lay next to me,
And I'm happy too,
To be in love with you,
No matter what I feel,
The love I feel is real,
No matter what people say,
I wouldn't give the time of day,
To sit and be with them,
When I can be with you and zen,
With only love in our atmosphere,
With you, our love is real.

-by Paige

All I See Is You Poem

Deep down true,
All I see is you,
You were meant for me,
True love will always be,
Ours, and our own love alone,
That no one else has ever known,
They think they know our lives,
But only we know what thrives,
Let them think they know something,
It's amusing to watch other beings,
Criticize and pass judgment,
Give their opinions, but we're above it,
We don't need to worry,
Forever is forever, we're in no hurry,
We will always be together,
Top of the list, above most others,
No matter what they think,
Or they tell, and become finks,
Of what they think they know,
Only we know how the true story goes,
How exciting is that?
Our own secret love pact,
No matter what they say,
Or whatever comes our way,
Only we know what is true,
All I see is you.

-by Paige

Everyone Wants to Be Loved Poem

Everyone wants to be loved,
It's a gift from Heaven above,
That not everyone knows yet,
But are waiting for, with no regrets,
For what they've had to go through,
Survive for, and endure,
Beat down doors and break rules,
For what they know is a precious jewel,
That's so rare and hard to find,
Like digging in a diamond mine,
They wait and live in a shell,
Hoping it will turn out well,
That someday they will be given,
The reason for they have been living,
To find their soulmate and love,
That will be theirs forever, here and above.

-by Paige

Sometimes You Just Feel a Connection Poem

Sometimes there are people you just connect to,
Right away, you feel they are like you,
You're so much the same, in so many ways,
You can't imagine not seeing them another day,
Maybe different in ways, but not many,
You're able to relate on the little, and the heavy,
Which you start talking about together, right away,
It's like you've known each other from long ago, another day,
You think the same way, and are some ways alike,
But in others ways, your own way, even though you might,
Do things or think the same, it all comes together,
Somehow you become, have, and will be connected forever,
You feel like there's something, it's like some magic glue,
It's awesome and strange, and they feel it too,
Even if some time passes, you still have that connection,
Between you and them, you both are a reflection.

-by Paige

You I Could Never Be Without Poem

You I could never be without,
For your love, I have absolutely no doubt,
Where that and your loyalty lies,
We have ties that bind,
Us together for eternity,
Apart, never will we be,
No matter where we are,
No matter how near or how far,
Nothing can ever come between,
What, to each of us, we mean,
And maybe no one else can understand,
The closeness, that you and I have,
But it doesn't matter in the least,
Together, our love will always reach,
Beyond anything else no matter what,
There is no limit of our love and trust,
It can be hard to find a love so strong,
That will last more than forever long,
But we are so lucky and so blessed,
That we have each other, to me, you are the best.

-by Paige

Will We Always Be Together Poem

Will we always be together?
Forever and ever?
I hope and I pray we will,
To be without you, I couldn't, never,

I wouldn't be the same without you,
As you wouldn't be without me,
We're just like peas in a pod,
We're as close as anyone could ever be,

I can't imagine the loneliness,
Of not knowing you as I do,
Even if I hadn't ever felt it before,
Something would be missing, without a clue,

Of letting me know where to look,
To find you so that I'm whole,
There would be a missing puzzle piece,
Not having a fit in my piece, would take its toll,

I'd be searching and I'd be scouring,
The whole world over for you,
Not knowing what I'm searching for,
My heart feeling sad and blue,

But we're so lucky we do have each other,
Somehow we just absolutely fit,
Each other's needs, wants and love,
Never ever change, not even a bit,

So I have to ask, and I have to know,
That we'll never be apart,
Forever and for all eternity,
You are a piece of my heart,

So will we always be together?
Always, forever and ever?
I know I don't have to guess,
I know the answer is yes.

-by Paige

Our Love Is Pure Poem

I know that our love is pure,
Of that, I'm absolutely sure,
Some may call it calm and plain,
But ours is a love that will remain,
It'll stay simple and sweet,
To each other, we can retreat,
And always be right there,
We never will despair,
For we know we're not alone,
To us, you and I are home,
The home deep in our hearts,
Knowing we'll never be apart,
We know we always have someone,
No matter what, to who, we can run,
When things turn upside down,
Or hardships come around,
Of course when good things happen,
We know the other will be clapping,
So we can't wait to tell each other,
About any happiness we discover,
Because we will be each other's,
Biggest cheerleaders of one another,
We will stand by each other's side,
Good or bad, we're along for the ride,
And will never leave, we know,
Like a seed into a tree, we grow,
And can get through anything,
Together, whatever life brings,
So thank you for being my best friend,
For you and I, there is no end.

-by Paige

What Would I Do Without You Poem

What would I do without you?
Honestly, I don't really know,
You make me want to be a better person,
You make me want to grow,

Into something more civilized,
And someone more than I am,
Into a more beautiful being,
Than I ever was to begin,

You don't even know how much,
You inspire me,
To be a better human,
Than I was born to be,

I'm so in love with you,
I'm in such high admiration,
For everything you are,
It's beyond my imagination,

Something I aspire to be,
Is as good as you,
You are my secret mentor,
Everything you are is true,

I'd be lost without you,
I admire you so much,
When they ask, "who's your hero?",
You are it, and nothing can touch,

The absolute inspiration,
Only you come near,
To whom I wish to follow,
It's so very clear,

You're who I want to emulate,
And follow your every lead,
With you in my life,
I have the guidance I need,

You're motivating more than you know,
And your spirit is contagious,
You give so much to this world,
Without knowing, you're beyond courageous.

-by Paige

In My Dreams Poem

Love is love,
For everyone,
Sometimes it's a little,
Or in the middle,
Sometimes it's a lot,
And sometimes not,
Even though you sleep,
Right here next to me,
Every single night,
I search for what feels right,
But suddenly it seems,
That in my dreams,
You are the one showing,
Before, faceless, not knowing,
Who was meant to be,
With me eternally,
We always think it's someone else,
And can't even trust ourselves,
Inside of our dreams,
We don't know what it means,
But once we see the face,
Every line that we can trace,
If our own true love,
That we didn't know was above,
Any faceless fantasy,
That we thought was meant to be,
Suddenly in my dreams,
Crazy it seems,
I can't get enough of you,
And tells me in life, to make it true,
Right in front of me,
How could I not see?
You will be my fantasy,
And what I choose to be,
My sweet true happiness,
Above any faceless guess,
You are real and mine,
My dream, I dreamt I'd find.

-by Paige

The One I Look Up To Poem

The one I look up to,
In everything that you do,
I'm simply amazed,
How you get through every day,
With such ease, no stress,
It seems so effortless,
Not letting things get to you,
Or being driven crazy by who knows who,
If you can't control it,
You never get upset,
You weigh things and are reasonable,
Everything is feasible,
You lead by example,
And give advice that matters,
You have discipline and work hard,
Never playing the sympathy card,
Knowing what has to get done,
And how to be independent as one,
Never needing help or a handout,
You wouldn't want that anyway no doubt,
You show such strength and perseverance,
You're not impulsive or ever frivolous,
I strive to be more like you,
My secret mentor, you're honest and true,
Never questioning your loyalty,
You are wise, witty, to me you're royalty,
In life you never know who you're inspiring,
Who's there watching and admiring,
So always know you're helping to shape,
Another one's life and traits,
For the good, and give them a lift,
To be more like you, would be such a gift.

-by Paige

Thank You for Loving Me Poem

I know sometimes it can't be easy,
For either of us, you or me,
There are so many ups and downs,
Obstacles we can't foresee,

But somehow and someway,
We've made it through to see another day,
Together, you and me,
Like I've hoped and prayed,

You are the one, who takes me away,
When I'm lost, and can't find my way,
I don't know, and forget who to trust,
Who's a true friend, and I become afraid,

But you, to my heart, are the key,
To be with you, I'm so lucky,
There are no other words or way to explain,
My love, thank you for loving me.

-by Paige

Friends for So Long Poem

How did we know,
We'd be friends for so long?
We didn't, and couldn't,
Knowing us, we were never wrong,

We were so alike,
And then became so different,
Adolescence, it happens,
We didn't know what it meant,

Because we were both confident,
In who we were and are,
And still strong in our ways,
Maybe that's why we've made it so far,

Mentally and physically,
We had that bond together,
Within us we both knew,
No ties could be severed,

Always laughing together,
Being there for one another,
Who knew the lifelong friendship,
That we had, was unlike any other?

We're alike, but like no other,
Both something truly special,
How we made such a friendship last,
Is actually kind of incredible,

How many friendships last this long?
I hope our story is never-ending,
Friends until the end and after,
Always there for one another, it's commending,

So no matter what we've been through,
And even though we're so different,
We're the same deep inside,
Each other, we truly compliment.

-by Paige

Inside My Treasured Chest Poem

I opened my heart for you,
It had been closed for so long,
Like a treasure locked in a wooden chest,
Until you came along,

Wounded and broken,
I had to lock it away,
And secretly hide the key,
For the right one to find someday,

No one could get to it,
It became cold and full of webs,
I wouldn't let anyone near,
It wouldn't be hurt again,

Safely it was kept,
No one knew it was there,
Wrapped tightly in a blanket,
Cradled with care,

Tucked away tight,
With hidden jewels and treasures,
Hiding ghosts from the past,
I'd preserve with great measure,

So guarded and protected,
Under heavy lock and key,
Almost as if it was dropped,
To the bottom of the sea,

Covered with barnacles,
Lost in the ocean,
Then you came to me,
And showed true devotion,

You lifted me from the depths,
Needing chains to bring me up, and retrieve,
Chipping slowly away at the lock,
Until it finally broke off, now love, I'm ready to receive,

And now that you've come along,
I've opened up my heart, inside of myself,
You broke in, saved and claimed it,
My heart, inside of my treasured chest.

-by Paige

You Heard My Cries at Night Poem

You heard my cries,
Deep in the night,
Where so many are alone,
And lay in fright,

We close our eyes tight,
Safely tucked away,
Hoping the sandman brings,
Only sweet dreams our way,

Of fairytales and gardens,
Covered with lovely dew and mist,
And fairies fluttering around,
Sprinkling their calming fairy dust,

Hearing sounds everywhere,
Pulling the covers up,
My minds eyes seeing shapes,
Maybe it's moondust,

Drifting me off slowly,
Lovely and sweet,
Dancing on the wall,
The moonbeams help me sleep,

Like a child seeing images,
I need you to hold me close,
So those appearances don't scare me,
So please never let me go,

Thank you for answering,
My cries in the night,
Now with your love to comfort me,
I know I'll be alright,

Holding me safe and warm,
Yours is the love I always want to know,
Just like my dreamcatcher takes nightmares,
I'll catch all of the kisses you blow,

No more cries at night,
And never again will that I go through,
I'm now able to sleep soundly,
Sweet dreams are because of you.

-by Paige

My Muse Poem

I love who you are,
And I love what you do,
Looking at you,
You are my muse,

You inspire me,
And give me strength,
To breathe again,
To dance in the rain,

Giving me freedom,
Through cloudy skies,
With your existence,
New beauties arise,

Feeling a newly found,
Peace again,
Being with you,
Now I can begin,

To put back together,
The broken pieces of me,
That didn't live anymore,
I didn't believe,

But you brought them back,
Together brand new,
The misplaced pieces,
With your secret gift, my muse.

-by Paige

I Can't Even Put Into Words Poem

I love you in a way,
I can't even put into words,
Nothing comes close to my feelings,
From anything I've ever heard,

No exact way to compare,
There's no identical description,
Of how my heart feels,
Or any way of true depiction,

It's so much bigger than anything,
And deeper than can be explained,
It's entrancing and overwhelming,
It takes over, pulling me by the reins,

There's no correct definition,
How much of my heart you've taken over,
It literally feels like it's grown bigger,
And you'll have all of it forever,

Because my love I feel for you,
Will never leave or be misplaced,
Is irreplaceable and stuck inside of me,
Unequivocally perfect, is the closest I can illustrate.

-by Paige

Animals Don't Care What You Have Poem

Animals don't care what you have,
As long as it's a love that lasts,
True and faithfully,
Beside you they'll always be,
As long as you're true to them,
Nothing is pretend,
They don't want your money,
Or worry they'll be hungry,
In your hands they feel trust,
Not caring even how you dress,
If you have makeup on or not,
Kisses will always be brought,
To your face, and hugs too,
No matter what you do,
As a job for a living,
As long as it's love you're giving,
Love they show back to you with cuddles,
And giving you sweet, close snuggles,
They will always be right there,
By your side, with true loving care,
That is undoubtedly real,
That's the only way they feel,
And you can trust that they will show,
Love back to you, that, you honestly know.

-by Paige

How Perfect Your Love is Meant to Be Poem

Love is never-ending,
Binding, or apprehensive,
You know when it's there,
You're always aware,
Right from the beginning,
It can leave your head spinning,
Not knowing what to make,
Of this love you'll never forsake,
This feeling that's spellbinding,
Is always worth finding,
And never letting go of,
This real, deep feeling of love,
That everyone dreams to find,
And what comes to in our minds,
Staking personal claim,
Is what we all want the same,
Someone who is our own,
That feels like, and becomes home,
Keep that wish and always want,
A love that you long to flaunt,
To anyone who can see,
Just how perfect your love is meant to be.

-by Paige

Could You Be the One Poem

Could you be the one?
That takes my blues away?
That makes me feel safe?
And makes me want to stay?

That I wonder about,
And where you are,
Do you really exist?
Are you very far?

Can people be happy?
And content?
At the same time,
With no regrets?

I think about it,
Why can't I have that also?
Some others seem to,
Why can't my dreams blossom?

Into reality,
Instead of just alone,
Inside of my head,
Where they're unknown,

To anyone else, only me,
Even though they stray,
From where I really am,
Wanting different, night and day,

Wondering if they'll come true,
Or just be fantasy,
Only time will tell,
What is truly meant to be.

-by Paige

I Want to Love Everyone Poem

I want to love everyone,
So many people are so good,
None of us are perfect,
But most, I think wish they could,

Be absolutely angelic,
In helping people and to engage,
Them in their darkest hours,
Giving them love that they've saved,

In a secret place,
Inside that no one sees,
It's there for safe keeping,
Like shadows in the trees,

With leaves to surround,
And cover them with love,
To nurture and keep them,
And give to the ones in need of,

Something to make them smile,
To make them happy inside,
And realize the days beauty,
Be glad that they're alive,

But we all know there are days,
We feel angry and jaded,
Nothing seems to help,
For us to escape it,

We wish we'd never gotten,
Up and out of bed,
Because nothing seems right,
Everything that's happening, we dread,

They can be hard to make it through,
Those days can be unbearable,
Watching every minute on the clock,
Lasting so long, the torture is terrible,

But step back for just a second,
Or longer if you need,
There are so many good people out there,
And they are the ones that feed,

Our hearts and our souls,
With love and understanding,
Being there, just because,
They're a decent human being,

We all have those days,
They come in different shapes and sizes,
Of the good, bad, and in between,
We never know what's to arise,

So look at things rationally,
Hopefully the day will come,
When we can all see with open eyes,
Because I so want to love everyone.

-by Paige

Chapter 2

<u>Love and Loss</u>

When I Close My Eyes Poem

When I close my eyes,
It's no surprise,
It's you I see,
Deep inside of me,
There's no release,
To move on or to freeze,
These feelings I have,
From the joy we had,
It doesn't fade away,
And I never will stray,
From your loving embrace,
I will forever retrace,
Every step we made,
None I would trade,
Every inch of your face,
No one could replace,
The love you've made me see,
I never thought could be,
But with you, it was real,
You forever, in my heart and soul, I'll feel.

-by Paige

A Love That Would Never Last Poem

I always wished for a love,
That would stand the test of time,
Two loves coming together,
Is what I dreamt I'd find,

I thought I'd found it in us,
It seemed so meant to be,
We would always be together,
In true love and harmony,

Little did I know though,
That what we have is strained,
Looking back it's so clear now,
I shouldn't have staked my claim,

Because unfortunately with love,
It can quickly fall apart,
No matter how much you put in,
Or how much you give of your heart,

I give everything I have,
But never did I foresee,
That you and I together,
Just weren't always meant to be,

I'll still try my very best,
And I'll give our love my all,
If it works then it's meant to be,
If not, my dreams of love will fall,

Because if you don't reciprocate,
And that's what will show is best,
To make me finally realize,
My love for you, I need to put to rest,

I'll know now to give up,
And know what is our true fate,
Not what I thought it would be,
Now our love and hearts are at stake,

I'll be so fragile and weary,
My heart will truly be broken,
My eyes will cry deep tears,
Because our love will be forsaken,

If it is though, I wish I'd known,
The love that would fade so fast,
And it can be gone so quickly,
In a love that would never last.

-by Paige

If I Could Do It Over Again Poem

If I could do it over again,
Everything I would mend,
And make it all right,
How torturous is hindsight?
If I were given another chance,
To change any circumstance,
That didn't seem right,
I would try with all my might,
To step back into the past,
And make it better at last,
If I could just go back in time,
Everything would be fine,
And you would know my love for you,
There's nothing for you I wouldn't do,
To make you see how I feel,
My love for you is so very real,
I hope you can see my truth,
I love you, always did, and do,
Because you're you, and you're precious,
To me, you're such a gift,
Please know you were, and are mine,
We will be together, for all of time.

-by Paige

It's So Hard to Live Without You Poem

It's so hard to live without you,
I see you in everything I do,
When a radio or something is on,
Or somewhere I hear a song,
That reminds me of you,
And the time that we knew,
Together and all my life,
It always makes me want to cry,
Or I may see something somewhere,
And it can absolutely tear,
My heart into pieces, and it aches,
Because it reminds me of you, and I just break,
Down, like the protective walls I try to have,
They fall, and I get upset and sad,
That you had to leave, because I wasn't ready,
And wanting you back is always heavy,
But I'll carry it, like in my heart, I carry you,
You always carried me, everything I went through,
You were always there and made it better,
No matter how stormy the weather,
I don't think I'll ever get used to,
Living in this world without you,
Memories come back in floods,
It can be so very tough,
To keep my composure,
Because when someone passes there's no closure,
And I would never want our love to close,
Beyond this earth our love forever goes,
It'll never disappear,
But without you here,
I don't know how I've gotten through things,
My heart and mind still clings,
To wanting you back, and to talk to you,
And everything that we used to do,
Wishing I could see you, and it could be,
Exactly like it was, and will be again eternally.

-by Paige

Why Into My Dreams Have You Crept Poem

After all that we went through,
I think I'm finally over you,
I delete all pictures and texts,
Throw things away, what's next?
I go without thinking about you,
I really feel I'm through,
And then there you are in a dream,
Better than it actually was it seems,
So real, happy and exciting,
Your touch and love, so inviting,
More lovingly real it even seems,
I don't even know what that means,
In my dreams we're so in love and sweet,
Entranced in each other's souls and beings,
It feels so real I don't want to wake up,
The tenderness is back, and we've made up,
It's nothing like when it came to an end,
And everything we had, felt like it was all pretend,
When you threw us away like trash,
Ripped up and unable to be patched,
You threw me for a loop,
Then into my dreams, you come in and swoop,
Me off of my feet, and I fall,
Back in love, but you're not really here at all,
Only when I'm asleep and unconscious,
You stroll back in, and I'm haunted,
I had moved on, and was on the mend,
And now here I go again,
Wishing we were still in touch,
Wanting to see you so much,
But if I saw you I know,
It wouldn't be like dreams show,
Things weren't nice when you left,
And so why into my dreams have you crept?
Back into my heart after you broke it,
After all the harsh, mean words that were spoken,
In my dreams, it's like you didn't up and leave me,
Without even giving me a reason,
I know when I'm awake you didn't really care,
So these "dreams" are more like a nightmare,
I don't like how I start to regress,
Become upset and get depressed,
I thought I was healed and fine,
Then right back to the beginning, you're on my mind,
Like a secret attack I didn't see,
I wish you'd go away and leave me be,

So I can move on with life,
Where you're not in my dreams at night,
I know the dreams are fake,
All along, we were wrong, what will it take?
To get you out of my head,
So I can dream again,
Of a love, one who's not you,
And fall asleep, with dreams of someone new,
But I will, because I'm strong I'll go on my own path,
And I will, get over you at last.

-by Paige

It's Funny How People Leave Poem

It's funny how people leave,
Even though you want to believe,
They were and are your friends,
But you always find out in the end,
If they're really there for you,
And to you, are really true,
If they're not, then walk away,
You'll find true ones someday,
Probably not when you look,
That's when it's real, it's all it took,
To show you that their friendship is real,
And you can most likely, deep inside, truly feel.

-by Paige

My Little Secret Poem

You were my little secret,
You, I can't forget,
At night, when I can't sleep,
You, in my head repeat,
I never will regret,
That you and I met,
For what we had,
I'm forever glad,
You were something I needed,
And then we proceeded,
Into an escape,
To a fantasy place,
It wasn't meant for forever,
Just for a moments pleasure,
Something uncertain,
Hidden behind a curtain,
Of fun, games and lies,
Then reality tried,
To let us know to stop,
Before the ball dropped,
I thought we could end nice,
But I should have thought twice,
Because feelings wouldn't have left,
The lust, we would have kept,
You turned on me in the end,
We can never begin again,
Now, I need to move on,
Back to where it is that I belong.

-by Paige

Without You I Can't Breathe Poem

Without you I can't breathe,
Why did you have to leave?
I'll never feel the same,
There's no one to blame,
My heart's been left wide open,
Indescribable words can't be spoken,
To possibly ever explain,
The severity of the pain,
That I feel within,
My heart is absolutely broken,
And nothing will heal the cracks,
Or replace you, that's a fact,
But I know we'll meet again,
I find it so hard to breathe, until then,
But I'll try my best, and know,
That you're still with me, everywhere I go.

-by Paige

I Was Never Alone Poem

To see an empty chair,
Worn out, well used, but now bare,
Is so incredibly hard,
You've gone so very far,
From where I can reach you,
You were always there for me I knew,
I was never alone,
To tears I'm now prone,
Constantly and not knowing,
When they'll come, showing,
My lonely grief,
That will never leave,
Wanting to talk to you but can't,
I can, but not hearing back causes panic,
The disconnect is beyond real,
And the emptiness that I feel,
Distance no one can see,
Is truly hard to believe,
Life can be so unfair,
So be in the present and more aware,
When we're all in life together,
As we will be again forever,
For now, let's never forget,
The memories, to preserve and protect,
They're beyond precious and safe,
In my heart and soul, you'll forever stay.

-by Paige

If My Heart Stops Poem

If my heart stops,
Don't worry, I won't,
I'll still be around,
You're not alone,

You can still reach me,
And I'm right by your side,
I'll never leave you,
I'm along for the ride,

We are still together,
Even though it doesn't seem,
I'll hear you when your whisper,
When you laugh, cry or scream,

Talk to me out loud,
And to my picture,
I'll try hard to answer back,
To show and let you know I'm listening,

And we'll be together again,
In a way that we both know,
Away from this odd separation,
And then we'll continue to grow,

But until then and that time,
Remember, I'm still with you,
Maybe even more so,
Through everything, it's me and you.

-by Paige

Chapter 3

<u>Emotions, Feelings and Coping</u>

The Emptiness You No Longer Crave Poem

It's always nice when you hear,
Something or someone to make it clear,
You're where you're supposed to be,
And everyone you simply cannot please,
They will ridicule,
Hang you,
Not asking questions,
No jury or selections,
Don't listen to them,
Listen to your freedom,
Not to be judged,
You're sentenced from above,
By your actions here on Earth,
They tell your true worth,
And love you no matter what,
From evilness, you are cut,
Just take your time,
And indefinitely you'll find,
What you needed and have saved,
For the emptiness you no longer crave.

-by Paige

No One Can Judge Until They're Perfect Poem

No one is perfect ever,
But people think they're so clever,
When they feel they can judge us,
Or have an opinion that's unjust,
They shouldn't be all that surprised,
They have no say in our personal lives,
Just as we don't in theirs,
We all have our own private cares,
It's not fair that they try to play,
This game of "they think they can say",
Anything they want or feel,
When they don't even know what's real,
Going on inside of our lives,
"Assuming", is just them spouting lies,
And we all deserve better than that,
We are the only ones who know the facts,
Just as they do about themselves,
It seems they just want to deflect and dwell,
On someone else's personal matters,
And try to create some chatter,
To make themselves feel better,
About what they personally weather,
To divert negativity from their own,
Bad vibes to which they are prone,
To have when they aren't in a good place,
That they don't want to, themselves, face,
But it's not fair for them to incriminate,
Or make up fibs, that's their mistake,
We all know our own truths,
So don't ever let them accuse,
You of anything made up they just want to,
Plain and simple, it's abuse,
No one should take that from anyone,
Or feel they are wrong or be shunned,
For living our lives our own way,
Just being our genuine selves day to day,
So don't ever let someone try to tell you,
How you should live, or what to do,
What they think is your right or wrong,
Well they can just move along,
And go their own way and deal,
With their own issues and not try to steal,
Anyone else's ways in life,
We know, for us, what is right,
Ignore them and never believe,
That anyone should follow someone else's lead,

Because for ourselves, we know what truly fits,
So no one can judge until they're perfect,
Which we all know is absolutely never,
Just go on with your life, in your own happy splendor.

-by Paige

Always Trust Your Gut Instinct Poem

Sometimes you hear a sound,
But it's not a sound that's actually around,
A voice maybe it seems,
But it's not really real, like in a dream,
It really is real though,
And deep down you know,
It's that voice inside of you,
That's there to guide you through,
You know it's your gut instinct,
That it's telling you to stop and think,
That something just isn't right,
You're filled with hesitation, maybe just a slight,
Sometimes more than a little though,
That's a sign telling you "No",
That something is simply wrong,
And you need to definitely move along,
Away from this imminent danger,
It could harshly be a life changer,
Don't ignore it, listen to this voice,
It's telling you and giving you a choice,
To listen to it and believe,
That you need to realize and leave,
The situation that you're in,
It's begging, so you can be the one that wins,
This messed up game being played,
That somehow you might be betrayed,
So to save yourself some grief,
And hopefully find great relief,
Listen, and do what it's telling you is right,
Don't hesitate, because you just might,
Get out of something bad happening,
Who knows what the next move might bring,
If you don't turn and run away,
Like your inner voice is trying to say,
Listen, because this is your secret link,
To be safe, always trust your gut instinct.

-by Paige

It's So Hard to Trust People Poem

It's so hard to trust people,
Even if we think they're friends,
A little time apart,
Shows it's easy to end,

You think you're so close,
Tell your secrets to them,
But when you're not around,
Those secrets somehow bend,

Into something entirely,
Not true or not real,
It's hard when it hits you right in the face,
How their reciprocation feels,

You feel so blindsided,
So slapped in the face,
You thought they were excited,
For the dreams you chased,

But once those dreams become real,
People show who they are,
They weren't really that excited,
For you to go too far,

With your hopes and dreams,
For a future so dear,
To your heart and soul,
They show how they really feel,

It may be difficult to see,
Or completely take grasp of,
But you have to believe,
They're not who you thought you loved,

So watch your back every second,
And every moment of your life,
Be happy, open, but aware,
It's hard to trust everyone you thought you might.

-by Paige

Feel Like You're Being Watched Poem

If you feel like you're being watched,
You need to somehow block,
Whatever it is, because you probably are,
Whether they're near, or whether they're far,
What you're feeling isn't fake,
And complete chaos it could create,
If you don't put up a safety net or a wall,
Remember, your gut instinct doesn't want you to fall,
So watch your surroundings, and be safe,
So that from any danger, you can escape,
Your intuition is real, and for a reason,
To keep you from harm, it's telling you, it's pleading,
To listen and watch, to get away from any threat,
If you do, with safety and peace you will be kept.

-by Paige

Never Give Up Poem

Never give up on yourself,
Or on anything that brings you wealth,
Wealth of any kind,
That's in your state of mind,
Of hoping and wishing for things,
We never know what tomorrow will bring,
It could have good or hardship,
But make it through, try not to slip,
Or fall, no matter what it brings,
It'll pass, and there's a new beginning,
The next day to rise above,
And feel the strength and love,
That surround you every moment,
Of every day, night, and to own it,
Own your strength and dignity,
And look deep inside yourself and see,
That what's inside you matters,
Forget any hostility or chatter,
It's time that it makes no difference,
We all deserve a second chance,
And we get that chance if we don't give up,
We'll all find our way to stay tough,
Inside of ourselves, and on the outside,
Face it, show no fear, no longer hide,
For we are all given this life to be,
Ourselves, no matter what, and to be happy.

-by Paige

It's Never Too Late Poem

No matter what situation you're in,
We all have a new chance to begin,
For ourselves, what we really want,
No longer will our feelings just taunt,
We all have the ability,
To become who we want to be,
No matter how big or how small,
Our secret wishes are ours standing tall,
Whatever we have to endure,
If we want it, we will for sure,
Tomorrow is always a new day,
To make changes going the better way,
Even if the road seems bumpy,
Or if it takes some time, while feeling empty,
Know that it can all be changed,
For our lives, we have the power to rearrange,
Anything and everything around us,
What we're going through, we have to trust,
That light will shine on us when it's time,
To make those changes and find,
That nothing stays the same,
Good or bad, only we will remain,
Inside we'll be stronger and better,
And that will last for us forever,
So remember, it's never too late,
To change, and make good things our fate.

-by Paige

Take Me as I Am Poem

Take me as I am,
And then I'll have no doubt,
How you really feel,
And what we're all about,

I may be different in ways,
Than others, but that's a given,
No one is ever the same,
Not one person, in the lives that we are living,

Everything in each of us is special,
In the ways that we act and we are, so never forget,
There's not one person out there,
That doesn't have some kind of unique effect,

We're all different, but still the same,
In that we all have our own qualities,
Even if not everyone appreciates them,
Beautiful and precious they'll always be,

Don't ever let someone tell you different,
Or let someone alter your mind,
They don't have the right if they try,
And they're wrong, if the good things in you they can't find,

We all have wonderful things to offer,
To ourselves, and to someone else,
So we all need to live our life our own way,
Everyone should, and is allowed to be themselves,

Honestly, it doesn't matter what others think,
If we're just us, and not hurting anyone,
We all have to be our own person,
If we were all the same, that would be no fun,

So let's embrace our differences and quirks,
And forget all of the naysayers,
Take yourself, and me as we are,
We will all be the answer to someone's prayers.

-by Paige

Listen to Your Head, and then Follow Your Heart Poem

Sometimes things are just so good,
We can't see past what's real,
We see what we want to see,
All we know is how we feel,

At times it is a good thing,
But other times, it may not be,
What we're really looking at,
What it is that we really see,

And other times it is just that,
The beauty right before our eyes,
We've waited and we've hoped for,
Now it's here, we fully realize,

But we have to look with our heads,
And not just with our hearts,
For we have to look at it clearly,
And definitely we have to be smart,

We need to be fully aware,
And look at the true situation,
Plainly see the true meaning,
Not be oblivious to any false creation,

That we may have made in our hearts,
Because we want it so much,
Not just be in a fantasy world,
That's finally within our touch,

It's right in front of us,
And it's right within our grasp,
But we have to listen to our heads as well,
For it may not be what we dreamed of at last,

So make sure that you look with open eyes,
Even with your heart pounding lust,
And see things as they are, good or not,
Listen to your head, and then follow your heart.

-by Paige

I Wish You'd Hold Me More Poem

I wish you'd hold me more,
No matter what I show,
What I know is I need you,
More than I've ever known,

More than I've wanted anyone,
Because I can feel it now,
Stronger than it's ever been,
I need you more now somehow,

I've felt lost without you,
Holding you so close,
It's what I realize now,
That I've missed the most,

I feel closest when I'm with you,
Than I've ever felt,
To be inside your arms,
Is what makes me melt,

I don't know how to ask for it,
And it's so hard for me to show it,
I wish I knew how to tell you,
In your arms, I feel a perfect fit,

I feel safe and warm,
Right where I'm supposed to be,
With me wrapped up in you,
And you wrapped up in me,

But what it makes me realize,
Is what I'm missing most,
Your love, I'm finally seeing,
Is love that almost froze,

To finally being where I want,
And exactly what I need,
Both of us together,
Growing love, from planting a seed,

I need that back again,
And somehow I'll find a way,
To show you how I secretly feel,
Because your love, and holding me, is our fate.

-by Paige

Vibes Can Transform You Poem

Do you ever feel,
Like vibes can transform you?
Just being in a different place,
You can be yourself so true,

Stop and just feel,
And think about what you're feeling,
Those vibes that are there,
May send you reeling,

Into a different place,
Somewhere unknown and scarce,
But it will make us be,
Aware and not scared, but fierce,

And feel what it means,
What it's showing in your soul,
To make you pure and real,
What's trying to make you whole,

Don't let it go,
Don't let it slip away,
Don't ignore what it's trying to tell you,
Today, and every day,

Everything that we believe,
Vibes that make us feel,
And make us who we are,
Vibes are what make us real.

-by Paige

Our Own Treasure Trove Poem

I'm so in love with me,
I'm the happiest I could be,
For what I love the most,
Definitely deserves a toast,
Because it's so rare to have,
So hard to find and grasp,
And hold onto so tightly,
It's right where it's supposed to be,
Something no one can touch,
Or take away I trust,
Because I know deep within me,
I'm who I want to be,
It's confidence and strength,
That nothing can ever taint,
It's mine, and mine alone,
You too can have your own,
If you truly believe,
In yourself and choose to see,
Exactly what you're made of,
A light will shine on you from above,
And show the beautiful creation,
That, sometimes takes patience,
To actually find and feel,
When you do, you'll know it's real,
You deserve only good and love,
And know that you are enough,
You don't have to be everything,
Just be yourself, and cling,
To knowing that always,
We can be free in our own ways,
Know that you are love,
That's our own treasure trove.

-by Paige

Do You Ever Feel Like You're All Alone Poem

Do you ever feel like you're all alone?
Like no one else has ever known?
That feeling that no one is there,
When people are around you, everywhere,
But none of them know how you feel,
And nothing seems like it can be real,
How could anyone else feel the same?
As me with my guilt, loneliness or shame?
Surrounded by absolute strangers,
Wondering when, or where in lies the danger,
Of someone finding out my secrets,
Or finding out my secret regrets,
Acting like the know me, or are my friend,
When they would turn on me in the end,
With no thought of how I'd be hurt,
Or caring what I felt of my worth,
How do I know who to trust?
My secrets with, or just,
Anything I want or feel,
I need to know who's really real,
It's so hard to let people in,
Where I hold my sacred secrets within,
It takes awhile, but if I do,
Let someone in, and there are so few,
But if you're one, please know I trust you,
Don't let me down, or I'll become further due,
To withdrawing, and holding myself deep inside,
And not letting new people know me, I'll hide,
If you're a part of this lonely unseen fate,
Don't be surprised, when time with you I no longer partake.

-by Paige

You're Beautiful, Know It Poem

You're beautiful, know it,
You're you, own it,
No one else can ever,
Copy you, so clever,
The ways they might try,
There's more deep down inside,
Of you to what people see,
No one can match your glee,
It shines out of your eyes,
And on your smile, it rides,
With beautiful buoyancy,
You're giving without even trying,
Showing the world your true being,
The love that the world is needing,
Your glow showers onto others,
And creates a presence that hovers,
Over you wherever you are,
And shines like a beckoning star,
Latching onto other beings,
Whether they know it or not, it's a feeling,
That they derive from you,
That only you can do,
We all have that glow to share,
And spread to others, so be aware,
That you are a star that shines bright,
In the dark and in the light,
And you could lead someone's day,
Into a happiness they won't want to stray,
Ever from, and you have helped someone else,
To unknowingly shine and glow themselves.

-by Paige

Things Only Change Can Bring Poem

I know that change,
Can often feel strange,
Everything's different,
Nothing seems in sync,
Everything's rearranged,
You can feel loneliness and pain,
Not knowing what to think,
Or where to find the missing link,
That will connect you back,
And get you on track,
With your old and new way,
And to see the light of day,
That seemed so long ago passed,
But it will come back at last,
Just know nothing stays the same,
Life can be a guessing game,
Of what move to make next,
Like strategic moves in chess,
Just trust and keep your faith,
That it'll be worth the wait,
Whatever is next in store,
For you could have so much more,
And gone will be the stress,
Of change you thought was a mess,
We all need to accept it,
And know if we'd kept it,
The way it was before,
Then we couldn't experience more,
Of new exciting things,
That only change can bring,
And bravely start a new routine,
So a beautiful new way can be seen.

-by Paige

The Little Creek That's So Serene Poem

The little creek that's so serene,
Where imagination and beauty is seen,
Water trickles across the rocks,
All time and chaos stops,
So quiet all around,
Only nature sounds are found,
Singing a melody,
Like it's only meant for me,
Calm and so tranquil,
It makes my heart feel full,
Of love for the simplicity,
Of what only nature can bring,
The sounds of leaves,
Rustling in the breeze,
And covered just enough by trees,
To let a gentle sunlight squeeze,
Through with it glowing rays,
Making it so easy to gaze,
At the waters rippling effect,
Where peace and love are met,
The animals with their sweet chirps,
The lullaby of the swirls,
Of all the natural sounds,
Where abundance of beauty is found,
Like your own secret place,
All negativity becomes erased,
And only love and light shine,
In to spray you with divine,
Calm and comfort to slow down,
From the bustle of the world around,
Here, only calm surrounds with each breath,
That you can take in at a new, cleansing depth.

-by Paige

You Think You Know People So Well Poem

Sometimes it's hard to tell,
You think you know people so well,
They are the ones you call your friends,
But are they there for you only in pretend?
You'll know when it comes to something,
Good or something troubling,
Happening in your life,
And you just need a friend in sight,
The ones who really are, will support,
Everything you do and not ignore,
When you prosper, or need a hand,
Like only a true friend can,
Without being jealous,
Or showing how callous,
They are of your success,
Or in your loneliness,
Whether it's for joy or comfort,
In your time of need, you won't have to wonder,
You may be surprised,
At who will rise,
And be the ones there for you,
Unlike the ones you thought you knew,
So never underestimate,
Or over create,
A friendship that is true,
For you both, in everything that you do.

-by Paige

I Made a Mistake Poem

I made a mistake,
In thinking you were my friend,
Not knowing you'd turn on me,
Or not be there for me in the end,

Of what I thought was a friendship,
And closeness that we had,
I was open and gave my true self,
Wishing now that I'd seen the bad,

Side of you that I didn't know,
Was actually under there,
Pretending you're so concerned,
Now I know you didn't care,

But I'm glad that I found out,
It's easier to let people go,
When you find out the truth,
Because then you really know,

Just who you can trust,
And not be fooled again,
By a fake, false person,
That never really was my friend,

A real friend is sincerely happy,
For you in everything that you do,
They won't ever turn their back,
They'll be there for you through and through,

I've found out that you won't,
And I guess you never were,
So from now on I'll always know,
And I'll always know to remember,

That you weren't really there for me,
And to not trust you again,
Because when it comes down to it,
You were never really my friend.

-by Paige

Animals Bring a Feeling of Zen Poem

Some people don't realize,
Just how special animals are,
They have this amazing ability,
To soothe you and beyond,

Just petting them can help,
Both of you and them,
It creates a healthy calm,
Brings you both a feeling of zen,

They just want to be loved,
And they just want to be touched,
That feeling that we all want,
To be adored so much,

They look at you with only love,
From way deep down inside,
For their feelings they show are real,
They're impossible for them to hide,

The true love that they feel,
And the true love that the give,
None of their feelings are fake,
That's just the way that they live,

So appreciate animals for everything they are,
Good, loyal and loving,
The affection that they want and give,
I wish more people were like them.

-by Paige

Finding Myself Poem

It's been quite a year,
Filled with happiness and cheer,
Ups and downs,
And facing fears,

Scary sometimes,
Exhilarating rides,
Not knowing what to do,
Thank God listening to my guides,

Learning and growing,
Scary changes showing,
Falling apart at times,
Self medication flowing,

Hoping no one can see,
How out of control I've come to be,
Lost and feeling alone,
Twists and turns, acting crazy,

Hating myself and crying,
To myself, and everyone hiding,
Not remembering things I do,
Messing up, covering up and lying,

Doing stupid things,
Bizarre texts, posts and messaging,
Embarrassed and having to fix,
But it was all still lingering,

Feeling like I fell down a rabbit hole,
Everything taking its toll,
Wanting off this crazy ride,
Of the bad, I need to let go,

Not knowing my fate,
Felt like I was eating off an empty plate,
Getting better can be harsh and hard,
Every day, is another day to wait,

Feeling like you've been dealt a raw deal,
And nobody knows how you feel,
The pain in your body and mind,
Like a mime, no one can understand or hear,

Then finally something clicks,
Like suddenly a light was switched,
Tried so many times before,
Now I'm ready to be fixed,

Slowly gaining strength and clarity,
It's hard to admit, but necessary,
Realizing what I really want,
Letting go of stress, and things not good for me,

No longer in denial,
Sometimes it takes more than awhile,
But when finally I was really ready,
Stress lifted, and my heart could smile,

Learning healthy goals,
Finally in control,
My heart's no longer heavy,
So happy I finally know,

Loving what I've been dealt,
And learning more about myself,
More about love and clean living,
Happiness, and caring about my health,

Making my dreams come true,
Being guided, reality is good,
Better than any lies,
Being strong like I knew I could,

Finally the courage to turn it around,
A new me I've found,
Holding on to what's important,
My feet on solid ground,

Now that my mind is clear,
Holding onto what I love so dear,
Being thankful for forgiveness,
Through so many tears,

And the precious kind of wealth,
Being able to forgive myself,
Those are the things that matter,
Appreciation and love above all else,

It's incredible to make a change,
Say goodbye to feeling deranged,
No matter how many times we've tried,
Ourselves we can rearrange,

Peacefully we can land,
And create a new life plan,
Positive thoughts and living,
Know it's possible and we can,

As we go there's a lot to learn,
To go back to normal we yearn,
After feeling horrible and defeated,
It's hard, but we can find the way to turn,

Myself, no longer I detest,
Fears and weakness I can put to rest,
Now I love me, since finding myself,
I love life more, and I feel blessed.

-by Paige

Let Anger Go Poem

Why can't I let anger go away?
And not ruin my plans for the day?
Why can't I just block,
The feelings and turn them off?
I hate being on this train,
With feelings of despair and pain,
Why can't I just derail?
And go a different trail?
It's not fair to let someone's actions,
Have such a profound reaction,
In my life, and my senses,
When what they did was senseless,
And they don't care to apologize,
Accept, or even recognize,
What they did to hurt me,
Or take accountability,
I wish, and want to let anger go,
I admire people who are able do so,
And walk with their heads held high,
Knowing they won't let evil or lies,
Hurt them anymore, in any way,
I hope I'm able to do that one day,
I want to be the one in control,
And never let someone make me cold,
I'll keep trying, so the pain will ease,
And I can move on and be at peace.

-by Paige

Breaking Through Poem

It's been so hard,
Seen things I didn't want,
Felt things I shouldn't,
They continue to try to taunt,

Why does this happen?
To ones that are good,
Only wanting sweet things,
Like everyone should,

But then, all of a sudden,
Something inside you breaks,
Your innocence and naivety,
It slowly crumbles, and takes,

It tries to take it, you feel crazy,
Alone, absent, going insane,
What and how long will it take?
To get away from the pain?

It's got to be within your reach,
You search and look everywhere,
Anything to help the pain go away,
Feeling sick inside, nauseous and bare,

With nothing to cover you up,
And make the bad things go away,
But help is there, just know it,
It takes awhile, but it'll be there someday,

Everyone has something,
Know that you're not alone,
Just wait another day,
From where you've been thrown,

It'll all come around,
And in your own defense,
You'll fight it and you'll win,
Breaking through that wicked fence.

-by Paige

I Want More Poem

No matter where I am,
Or in my life, it seems I've been,
I always seem to want more,
Than I have been given,

I'm looking for something else,
I always seem to be searching,
There must be more out there,
To satisfy my yearning,

For more than what I have,
Looking beyond my reach,
Not knowing what I'm looking for,
I keep dreaming about, and seek,

For more than what I want,
But I don't even know what that is,
What lies out there hidden?
The secret for my happiness,

Why can't I just be happy?
With what I already have,
Most people would be thankful,
Grateful, and so glad,

I need to stop thinking,
That there's more to what I've got,
I need to be more content,
Because actually, I have a lot,

That others might want,
And see as a gift,
I too should see it that way,
For what I have is actually priceless,

Because no matter how much,
I have, or where I live,
I have more than so many,
Especially if I have extra to give,

I'll look more at what I have,
Turn my thinking around,
I have so much to be thankful for,
Happiness is here to be found,

I will open my eyes and mind more,
And see that I'm blessed beyond measure,
We all have our own things in life,
That we need to appreciate more, and treasure.

-by Paige

You Shake Me to My Core Poem

Sometimes you shake me to my core,
Don't make me think you're a chore,
With things you do to hurt me,
These games, confusing me mentally,
I feel deserted and distorted,
Tangled in a web and contorted,
Playing with my feelings,
Emotions sending me reeling,
Into a place of unknown,
Where I don't know what's right or what's wrong,
Sometimes I don't think I can take anymore,
And there you are, showing up at my door,
And I let my guard down,
Because you, I love to be around,
Even when I don't mean to, it seems,
And there's nothing else for me to cling,
Onto, because with you, I'm defenseless,
I feel drawn to you, and then I'm helpless,
So don't ever be a nuisance,
With false feelings that are useless,
And mean nothing real,
Flustered you make me feel,
Be nice to my heart,
If you don't want to be apart,
Because it can be yours for the taking,
As long as you don't break it.

-by Paige

We're All Trying Poem

We're all trying,
To make our way,
Every moment,
Of every day,

When things don't go,
As we planned,
Sometimes we reach,
For a helping hand,

We have it in us,
To make it through,
Giving up,
Is something not to do,

Even if our goals,
Take days, weeks or years,
Are filled with happiness,
Or frustration and tears,

We will get through,
And we will surpass,
The roadblocks we come upon,
We will get past them at last,

But no matter what,
Don't ever give up,
You'll reap the rewards,
You deserve every bit of,

And you'll be so proud of yourself,
You didn't go this far,
To be kicked to the curb,
By anything, you'll spar,

Whatever gets in your path,
Or tries to detour,
Or stop you in any way,
This destination is yours,

So remember, we're all trying,
Even on days we feel depleted,
We're all the same and fighting,
We cannot be defeated,

So know you're not alone,
And whether you have a little help,
You will be successful,
Ultimately, you did it yourself.

-by Paige

Jealousy is Worthless Poem

Jealousy, just shouldn't be,
There's no competition between you and me,
You do your thing, I'll do mine,
Each of our ways, is perfectly fine,
I'm happy for you,
In everything you do,
Be happy for everyone,
Because when the day is done,
We will all still be us,
To be jealous is ridiculous,
And a waste of time,
It's just a state of mind,
That you can toss away, and love,
Everything that you are made of,
Don't want what's not yours,
What people have could be better or worse,
No one is, or has, the same,
We're all beautiful in different ways,
Successful in everything we do,
Because it's only our own eyes we look through,
So be thankful that you're you,
And let others be themselves too,
Because no one will ever have the same,
And no one is to blame,
Because we all have our own lives to live,
Jealous feelings, you need to rid,
Yourself of, because they serve no purpose,
Jealousy, is just worthless,
We are all unique and special,
And in our own traits, simply revel,
In being just ourselves,
And like nobody else,
With what you've been given,
In your life that you are living,
We're all beautifully created,
And we should be individually celebrated,
So try to never be jealous,
And just be you, at your very best.

-by Paige

See What's Right in Front of Your Face Poem

You don't have to know everything,
Or even be a genius,
When scary things are happening,
And when a situation is heinous,

Staring right at you,
Right in the face,
It can happen so fast,
Dangerous, it may be the case,

Chaos can happen,
So quick you won't remember,
Who did, or said what,
Facts laying in the smoldering embers,

And people will lie,
To cover and save themselves,
Or stick up for their friends,
Whether it's the truth or not they tell,

When you're not looking,
Vicious people can attack,
When you're all alone,
And no one's there to have your back,

See people for who they are,
Really look at them close,
Some may try to hide things,
But you can see what shows most,

Study their every move,
Be intuitive and watch how they act,
With keen perception,
You'll be able to tell pretty fast,

And if you notice they're not good for you,
By things they do and say,
Get out and away from them quickly,
Learn to see what's right in front of your face.

-by Paige

I Fell Down Poem

I fell down,
I couldn't get back up or even sit,
The pain hurt so badly,
And everything came down with it,

When you fall,
Sometimes you don't want to get back up,
You feel like there's nothing left,
Inside of your loving cup,

It's empty and hard,
Dried out and stained,
Nothing could clean it,
The pain stains remained,

Just to walk,
The struggle was real,
Nobody else,
Can feel the pain that you feel,

Even if they've gone through similar,
Times, and similar feelings,
We all feel things differently,
There's no right or wrong in our healings,

So don't ever put someone down,
Or judge in any way,
How someone gets through something,
And goes on from day to day,

Just be there for each other,
And always have empathy,
Let people mend in their own ways,
That's how it is, and how it should be.

-by Paige

When Someone Lies Poem

When someone lies,
It's hard to begin,
To trust them,
And believe them again,

Tried for so long,
To believe their lies,
Wanted to,
Even though it was no surprise,

It makes you sick inside,
Literally more than you thought,
Could ever be real,
The agony they brought,

They don't know,
What they've done,
The damage they did,
How bad memories flood,

And once you find out,
If they want to make it right,
It's constant agony,
And constantly a fight,

But if they really are,
Sorry, and were lost,
Remember, we're all human,
We don't realize the cost,

Of all of our actions,
At that very time,
Even if they've been there for a long while,
There's no reason or rhyme,

We're all human,
And people get in a place,
Of being lost,
Not knowing what we'll face,

The arguments and hate,
Not believing the truth,
All you want,
Is to get back your youth,

Of the time you feel was wasted,
On this person that you love,
And trusted so much,
Thought you fit just like a glove,

I didn't think it was possible,
But you actually can,
Get back to normal,
When something hits the fan,

If it takes you showing them,
And blows back in their face,
They're able to see,
What they almost erased,

Until they're really ready,
And sorry for what they've done,
Until it's done to them,
They don't realize, it's not fun,

Sometimes you have,
To fight fire with fire,
Or they won't realize,
They can lose you, and be in dire,

Issues with you,
That's when they realize,
You too can move on,
And now who cries?

If you stay together,
Be able to provide proof,
Of what is real,
And what is the truth.

-by Paige

Instead of Getting Mad or Upset Poem

Instead of getting mad or upset,
I've decided I'm just going to let,
Things go that bother me,
Let them roll off my sleeve,
Without needing a crutch or escape,
Just walk away, and stay away,
From people they are mean and rude,
Malicious, disrespectful or crude,
Just take deep breaths,
Let it go and just rest,
It's not my problem, it's theirs,
For not me, but them to repair,
And let them go from my life,
Cut off all contact and be wise,
Taking care of me,
And my own mentality,
Get them out of my thoughts,
Where they would just taunt,
Don't dwell on it, let it go,
So I can have my peaceful flow,
And again I can find,
My sanity and peace of mind,
Be glad they're out of my life,
Causing me no more strife,
Sometimes we have to be done,
You have to turn your back on some,
And each go our own way,
So we can be at peace in our days.

-by Paige

Let Me Forget That Me Poem

Come take me away,
With you I want to stay,
Somewhere deep in refuge,
Don't let me refuse,
Because I need to be,
Awoken, and set free,
From the chains hiding,
That no one can see binding,
Wake me up my love,
Free me, from who I was,
And maybe then,
I can begin again,
In this world,
With brand new fuel,
Please take care of me,
Let me forget that me,
That couldn't take care,
And wasn't aware,
Of just how to live,
In the life I was given,
I want to break away,
No longer afraid,
Take me with you,
Don't leave, hopefully you won't want to,
Torn and frayed,
I need you to save,
Me and who I am,
Only with you, I can begin again.

-by Paige

Like a Sleeping Beauty Poem

I've been so tired,
Can't keep my eyes open,
Like a sleeping beauty,
One day I'll awake, I'm hoping,

It's like a spell was cast,
Too hard to stay awake,
This slumber I feel,
I can't seem to shake,

I just want to fall,
Crumble to the ground,
But I would stay there,
If no one was around,

I can't hold myself up,
Or hold my thoughts together,
Maybe it's just me,
Or maybe I'm under the weather,

They say to be strong,
But listen if your body needs rest,
Must I push on?
I'll listen to what's best,

I wish I could be awake,
Like everyone else seems,
When I sleep, I have nightmares,
And I just want to sweetly dream,

The bad dreams don't even wake me,
I have to fight dragons in them,
And then once they're gone,
Another one comes again,

Tossing and turning,
Why can't I find a prince?
To come and save me,
Who will wake me with a kiss,

And feel like myself again,
Instead, there's no one to hold,
I pull the blankets up tight,
But still, a feeling of cold,

Why can't I be awake when I should?
And asleep only when I'm supposed to be?
This sleeping beauty is tired,
Wake me sweetly, or let me sleep as long as I need.

-by Paige

If You Feel the Need to Scream Poem

If you feel need to scream,
Don't hold it inside,
Where it makes you literally sick,
And where it boils and hides,

Let it out somehow,
But in a good, healthy way,
Find an outlet for yourself,
Where you won't feel like prey,

We all have those feelings,
And sometimes don't know what to do,
Don't let them fester or ruin,
Anything that brings happiness to you,

Because that can often happen,
When we don't find a sane release,
We can take it out on the love we know,
When all we want to find is peace,

Keep it far from your loved ones,
Those relationships, don't compromise,
They will be the ones there for you,
During and after, you will realize,

Just who stays, and who doesn't,
And if they don't, they didn't matter,
Let, and allow, yourself to be free,
Of any torturous, inside chatter.

-by Paige

Can I Trust You Poem

Can I trust you?
To be true,
To the words,
That I heard,
They came from you,
Now I feel like a fool,
But I know I'm not,
Apparently like you thought,
To my surprise,
You were full of lies,
Sounding sincere,
Not realizing danger was near,
Maybe I was naive,
What you said I believed,
But I trust people first,
Until they turn for the worst,
Just be straight with me,
Because I can turn and leave,
Feeling like I've been betrayed,
Now I see through, I was prey,
And now I'm jaded,
My trust has faded,
You've made me suspicious,
Of people I don't know being malicious,
I was just being myself,
While you were planning something else,
And I got served a raw dish,
Feeling blindsided and foolish,
So don't expect me to stay,
And play your silly games,
I'll be on my way,
Only with people I trust will I stay.

-by Paige

Chapter 4

<u>Strength, Courage and Healing</u>

Everything Can Be Fixed Poem

No matter what breaks,
It can be fixed,
Maybe with superglue,
Or prayers instead, that's a better mix,

The angels are real, we all know,
Even if some don't admit,
They help us through everything,
We couldn't survive without them, not a bit,

Everyone is strong, some more than others,
But we all feel it deep down inside,
The strength we have, some not until we need,
To show it, it explodes from where it hides,

We all have it, there's no doubt,
We're all strong and we can kick,
All of our problems to the curb,
For real, everything can be fixed.

-by Paige

Why Would You Let Someone Bring You Down Poem

Why would you let someone bring you down?
They don't have the right to,
They don't have the power to either,
Unless you let them take it from you,

It is easy for them to take it though,
But we have to be strong and smart,
No one ever can take something away,
That's inside you, deep in your heart,

And also deep inside your soul,
You, and only you, hold that key,
A key that's not material, but real,
Something no one else can see,

It's much more powerful than they know,
And maybe even more than you do yourself,
But it's there, and it's not up for grabs,
It's yours alone, don't give in to their stealth,

Always be cautious and careful,
Always stand tall and be proud,
They can't hurt you, so don't ever let them,
They really can't, so believe it, they're not allowed.

-by Paige

When You Need Fixing Poem

You've been fighting it so long,
If it's messing with your life,
You know it's time for a change,
And the tears you can finally wipe,

It could be from anything,
Some are necessary to survive,
From alcohol, or food, to medicine,
Some are things you need to stay alive,

It's not your fault, it happens,
Some you need, and some may help,
And some you can't stop for reasons,
Without them, it can be harmful instead,

It can be challenging at times,
But you've got to stay strong,
You have the control now,
Don't let it go, keep holding on,

You will win this race,
And get to the finish line,
But give yourself a break,
It all takes time,

You can want something so much,
It seems so easy to grasp,
But it's so easy to fall back,
Anyone can have a relapse,

Just pick yourself back up,
And dust yourself off,
Don't beat yourself up,
Don't count it as a loss,

Just start again,
However many times you need,
As long as you're trying,
You will eventually succeed,

In fighting off the bad traits,
They will be gone at last,
If you never give up,
The wickedness will pass,

No one is ever perfect,
We all have our own struggles,
With everything in life,
We have to learn how to juggle,

And learn to handle things,
Without a coping mechanism,
But with peace, love and understanding,
To your heart and soul, just listen,

Because you know you want to get better,
And know you can definitely be fixed,
No matter how long it takes, keep working at it,
You'll overcome it and win the gold, you've got this.

-by Paige

Do You Really Think Someone Could Hurt You Poem

Do you really think someone could hurt you?
They have absolutely no right,
To try to take anything away from you,
They have no power, make them feel fright,

They can't ever get to you,
So don't ever let them near,
Inside or outside they'll try,
But you hold the power, it's clear,

They can't really get to you,
In any sort of way,
No matter what kind the try,
Their tactics will stagger and cave,

Or nor matter who they have,
That's standing by their side,
Once you let yourself be known,
No longer will your confidence hide,

But that's alright if even you,
Aren't quite yet able to see it,
Fake it, for your strength inside,
Will show, and you'll be able to feel it,

Even when you feel helpless,
Or even if you feel weak,
Give a smirk in your smile,
Whether it's helpless, or helps you to seek,

The words that you wish,
Would show up right away,
To show that you're not scared,
And shout that you're not prey,

Because you own your own self,
You, and nobody else,
Know it and believe it,
They can't take it, you showed the cards you dealt,

And the safety you hope to find,
Along with others out there,
Will help to clear your mind,
To show no fear, and stay aware,

Don't ever let someone hurt you,
Or take anything away that's yours,
You're strong, you own that power,
It's yours, you will last and endure.

-by Paige

This Too Shall Pass Poem

No matter what life deals,
We all have obstacles,
Challenges to face,
They can feel impossible,

We all have things we go through,
We have to find a way,
To try to stand tall and make it,
Every day, and to the next day,

They're always different it seems,
It can feel unbearable,
Everyone has things to face,
But they can't make us unstoppable,

It's hard that it sometimes takes this,
To force and make us stronger,
But it will in the long run,
And then anything we can conquer,

Because we will know how to face,
And look fear in the eyes,
And say straight to it,
We will be strong and rise,

Above the troubled times,
And beyond the wicked face,
Of anything trying to take us down,
Fear will be erased,

Some times are more difficult,
And harder than most others,
But we have it somewhere deep,
Inside where both fear, and butterflies, flutter,

It may take some time,
So give yourself a break,
You can take as much time,
As you need to take,

It's no one else's business,
And no one can tell or judge,
You, or when you should feel better,
Only time will help soften the edges,

So don't listen to others opinions,
Just know, bad times don't last,
Somehow, some way, life goes on,
And know sweetly, this too shall pass.

-by Paige

Difficult Times Can Be a Blessing Poem

I know it sounds weird,
But sometimes when things are hard,
They can actually be a blessing,
You may have been dealt an ace card,

When everything turns against you,
And you feel lost in every way,
It can mean that something better,
Is meant for you a new day,

It's hard when things hit you,
In an uncomfortable situation,
But you are meant for better things,
It all comes unseen, and with patience,

There's no one that doesn't get them,
Life is so hard at times,
Absolutely nothing makes sense,
With no reason or rhyme,

But then down the road,
You see that shining light,
It may take awhile,
There's no time limit in sight,

So just go along,
With the hand that you've been dealt,
I know, it can be hard, and sad,
But someday, happiness will be felt,

We don't know which way to turn,
And we may turn a lot of ways,
Trying to find the mixture,
Of what is to become of our days,

But Divine Guidance will show,
All of us beyond reasoning,
It's hard to see, but we will,
Difficult times can be a blessing.

-by Paige

The Only Me That Will Ever Be Poem

I know I have some quirks,
And things may be odd people see,
I know I'm not perfect,
But I'm the only "me" that will ever be,

I have some little habits,
We all do you know,
Different from others,
Sometimes they do or don't show,

But we're all alright, just know,
I wouldn't want to be anything else,
No matter how different we are,
I was made to be me, I'm myself,

And you shouldn't want to either,
Be anyone else and not you,
No one should want to change who they are,
We're all unique and of value,

Don't ever underestimate,
What you mean to people,
Always remember this,
We are all irreplaceable,

And you owe it to yourself,
Whether you see it or not,
You need to know and honor this,
The person you are, soul and heart,

You're the only you,
That will ever be,
So realize your rareness,
And love your own specialties,

For you are the only one to offer,
Just as I am, our own qualities,
These are what make us stand out,
In our own beautiful individuality,

We're all original and great,
And everyone needs to accept,
What we each have to offer,
Without feeling contrite or regret,

What we all have, of our own things,
That others might think are peculiar,
But we all need to understand,
And welcome each other for who we are,

No one is bizarre or strange,
Or so different than you or me,
No matter what quirks we have,
We all are the only "us" that will ever be.

-by Paige

Don't Underestimate Me Poem

Don't underestimate me,
Or make me make you see,
Just how strong I am, and able,
And just how much I'm capable,
Of taking care of myself,
I thought I did, but don't need anyone else,
To take my hand or show me,
How to be independent and free,
Somehow I'll find my own way,
I don't know what hour or what day,
But I do know those shoes I can fill,
Because my strength is as strong as my will,
So don't ever take me for a fool,
That can be disenchanted by you,
I will stand on my own,
And I will let that be known.

-by Paige

Don't Hold on to People Who Have Let You Go Poem

Sometimes people have to leave,
Even if they don't want to,
So deep down in our hearts and memories,
Those are the ones to hold onto,

But when others are deliberate,
And are just able to up and leave,
Without a goodbye or a reason,
Try not to, for very long, grieve,

Because even though it seemed real,
They were never really there,
Unlike the ones who had to go,
Only those are ones to hold forever dear,

If it wasn't their choice to leave,
Dearly they still hold you too,
Just as tight as before,
Those are the ones who are true,

Unfortunately, the ones who chose to leave,
And ghost you like you weren't wanted,
Once you're able to let them go,
No longer will you be haunted,

By the memory of only lies,
Of someone still here, but not,
If they didn't care to stay,
Use the lessons that it taught,

No matter how many tears you've cried,
Remember you were taken for granted,
They weren't right for you to begin with,
Or their love wouldn't be so easily recanted,

They don't deserve you, or to know,
Any pain that they made,
It may take a while, but that's alright,
You'll be better off in every way,

Even if it doesn't feel like that right away,
Or no matter how long it takes,
Keep your dignity and always know,
You have a new life to create,

Someday you'll find, in your heart and mind,
With letting them go it's a release,
It will actually feel good and empowering,
And you'll find an inner strength and peace,

That relief of letting them go,
You'll be amazed and surprised,
Being able to rid all reminders,
You'll feel renewed and so wise,

So when you're ready, move on,
And only keep the ones that you should,
For they are with you no matter what,
They are the only ones, for you, that are good,

Don't hold on to people who have let you go,
When you let go, you'll feel a sense of calm,
The serenity of being set free,
What you've needed, and wanted, for so long.

-by Paige

Do What's Right for Yourself Poem

Do what's right for yourself,
It's the only way you're going to help,
Ease any pain,
And keep you sane,
It has to be right for you,
Not what anyone tells you to do,
You get to make the decision,
And no one is allowed to question,
How you choose to deal,
With how things make you feel,
Find a good way to have less stress,
Whether it's by forgiveness,
Or by walking away,
After being betrayed,
It's all up to you,
But see it from a healthy view,
As a way to help you heal,
From any pain or sadness you feel,
There's no one you need to ask,
And no longer do you need to mask,
Any heartaches that hurt,
Happiness and serenity you deserve,
So do what feels right for you,
The direction is yours to choose,
And then stand tall and be proud,
Because a new clean slate you have found.

-by Paige

There's a Lot I Can Take Poem

There's a lot I can take,
Make no mistake,
But until you see your own reflection,
Everything is a distorted depiction,
Of what the truth really is, and actually,
You know it as well as I do, factually,
Correct, and proven over and over again,
So distance will be the only way to mend,
Because if you can't see it, I can't show you,
You have to see it in your own view,
The truth of how you treat me,
And how it naturally should be,
Honest, loyal and true,
Instead of wondering if I've been lied to,
And stabbed in the back again,
We make up, and I don't know if it's pretend,
I never know where I stand with you,
But playing mind games, I'm through,
Like secrets pulled from a wooden chest,
You've thrown at me, and have lost my trust,
Then I try to give it another chance,
Just to be in a state of trance,
Everything seems so normal in pictures,
But behind the scenes, it's all fiction,
I don't know what else to say,
Or try to makes things okay,
Because from that same chest, popped the latch,
And suddenly I felt detached,
The freedom that I'd waited to find,
Spilled out all over, and it was mine,
I'll be cordial, and I'll still care,
From a little and afar, so be aware,
And remember, there's a lot I can take,
I've learned to bend, but I won't break.

-by Paige

Back to Me Poem

It's been a long time,
Since I've felt fine,
I've been through a lot,
Feeling cold, and then hot,
My head spinning out of sorts,
Trying to get back on course,
With who I used to be,
And finally get back to me,
It's been a hard journey,
Twists and turns I couldn't see,
Crashed a few times,
I couldn't stay in line,
I sped, slipped and fell,
Waiting for time to tell,
When, better, everything would be,
And finally get back to me,
I've begged and I've pleaded,
For healing so much needed,
And for things to become easier,
Sometimes it didn't seem feasible,
But somewhere along the way,
I don't even remember the day,
Somehow I was given a lift,
And inside, I didn't feel such a rift,
A load was taken off of my shoulders,
Mentally, and physically, less colder,
Not so much heavy turmoil,
Or feeling like I was coming to a boil,
The mending then took time,
But at last, freedom inside was mine,
And now, beautifully I see,
I'm finally back to me.

-by Paige

Handle Everything with Grace Poem

When life breaks you down,
And it feels like no one's around,
To help you up, or to give,
A hand to you as a gift,
To pull you out of the trenches,
Where you can feel so small and helpless,
And lift your spirits up,
When they're feeling rough,
Know that even if no one's there,
There are always people who care,
But care enough about yourself,
Because you are your own best help,
To pull yourself up and out,
Of any ditch where you've been thrown about,
You have the power, strength and will,
To gracefully pull yourself up the hill,
All by yourself, with dignity,
Knowing you didn't need anyone to lead,
You'll take pleasure in knowing how you can,
Handle things thrown at you, with elegance,
And pure charm in your own way,
Those dragons that hurt you, you will slay,
So take charge, but go at your own pace,
And learn to handle everything with grace.

-by Paige

Be in Love with Life Poem

When things are good it's easy,
Everything is so pretty,
But it doesn't always stay like that,
Unfortunately things can take a step back,
And they will because it's inevitable,
How life changes, it can be unbelievable,
One day good, one day bad,
One you're happy, the next you're going mad,
So when the days are good, really notice,
Learn how to soak it all in,
Relish in it, hold the good close and tight,
Because someday, you may need it to fight,
Off the bad, that's looming overhead,
And you wish you'd never gotten out of bed,
But you have to get up and keep going,
And move on in life by knowing,
That bad times don't ever last,
They will go, maybe slowly, but will surely pass,
So when they happen, remember the good times,
Be in love with life, because you'll always find,
Something you can smile and revel in,
That can make you happy again,
Just thoughtfully use the lessons you've learned,
And appreciate them, by savoring the joys that you've earned.

-by Paige

Set Me Free Poem

Set me free from this craziness,
Until then, it's hard to rest,
From these chains that bind,
Me, to an age and time,
Where I don't feel I am anymore,
I've walked through another door,
And moved on to another place,
From where I was, I couldn't stay,
I've opened up my mind,
Yet saved it at the same time,
To return to my existence,
No matter how resistant,
My mind tried to be,
Finally I can see,
Through my thinking, heart and soul,
Only I, yet so many people, know,
Just how hard it is,
And just how torturous,
It is to find yourself again, and be,
Your real you, and finally break free.

-by Paige

The Lotus Poem

Through sludge and mud,
I will arise,
To start again,
To my surprise,

Or maybe yours,
You didn't know,
Covered in dirt,
That I would show,

Just how strong,
I could be,
Not only you,
But I couldn't see,

And now I can,
Thank you for that,
You helped me out,
Imagine that,

I'd never have known,
What I was made of,
You helped me grow,
When push came to shove,

I needed that,
No matter my hurt,
To rise back up,
What I gained, it was worth,

So like the lotus, I will submerge,
Out of mud and pain,
And again I'll be strong,
Of me, I will reign.

-by Paige

Never Let Your Guard Down Poem

Never let your guard down,
Where threats can be found,
Danger can always be around,

Stay safe and be aware,
And never show fear,
No matter how far, or how near,

It is from you,
Do what you have to do,
Be strong, and be wise too,

Remember to stand tough,
Even when times are rough,
Know that you mean so much,

To you and your loved ones,
When push comes to shove,
Invisibly put on your boxing gloves,

And fight with all that you have,
No matter what, you'll be glad,
That you did just that,

Some mean people think they're so clever,
But goodness, you will endeavor,
So never let your guard down, not ever.

-by Paige

In the Dark Howling Wind Poem

The wind is howling,
While I lay in my bed,
As the beginning of dreams,
Swirl in my head,

It sounds so fierce,
So strong and mean,
But I know it can't hurt me,
It can't even by seen,

Once it gets late,
It's very strange,
How different it feels,
Like everything's changed,

Is there something out there?
Something I dread?
Or is it inside?
Maybe under my bed?

No, there's not anything,
That can hurt me here,
It's just my imagination,
The coast is actually clear,

So I need to realize,
And I need to clear my thoughts,
Of thinking unnecessary things,
That aren't even real to haunt,

Me or anyone else,
In the dark and still of the night,
It's quiet, but hearing sounds,
Just waiting for the light,

Our minds go overboard,
And get too carried away,
When it's nighttime, by ourselves,
Waiting for the next day,

The darkness seems cold,
But not in temperature,
More like alone,
And feeling vulnerable,

I know in the dark,
What I think might be,
But if I can't see it,
Then it can't see me,

If I listen closely,
I can hear there's nothing to fright,
For it's just nature whistling,
And I know I'll be alright.

-by Paige

What is it That You Need Poem

What is it that you need?
To feel like you succeed,
In this life you're living,
With all that you've been given,
Is it something that deals with love?
Like needing a message from above?
Or maybe with your work,
That'd take away stress and hurt,
Whether it be emotional strain,
Or possibly a physical pain,
Do you want something better?
Are you feeling under the weather?
Maybe it's friends or family,
And the chaos it can carry,
When people aren't getting along,
Being in the middle of right and wrong,
Accused of taking sides,
Or accused of someone's vicious lies,
Maybe you don't even know them,
But they present themselves on a whim,
And if it's not something good,
Or working out like it should,
You end up taking the blame,
No one should be allowed to dirty your name,
So if you find yourself wanting more,
Move on and through a new door,
Find out what's inside,
The secrets to prosperity that often hide,
Where we can't always see,
And seem far beyond our reach,
Then you can take a step back,
From the turmoil, you can finally relax,
And are able to find happiness,
For yourself, and let go of the rest.

-by Paige

Liberating Poem

I'm no longer interested,
In going back or regressing,
To being around anybody,
That makes drama a hobby,
If they don't want anything to do with me,
That's fine, I'm able to plainly see,
What's written on the wall,
And without them, I won't break or fall,
Because I can't let someone take,
Or, make me, partake,
In any negativity,
It makes me actually feel free,
To move on and ignore,
And not be a part of their war,
Just let them go,
The distance between you will show,
A new and powerful light,
Like a beacon in the night,
Call it growing up, or just being smart,
It really is a true art,
To choose to be happy and thrive,
And letting go of hatred in my life,
Tidying up my thoughts and sense,
Of well-being, without feeling spent,
So if you feel malice from someone,
Choose to love yourself and you'll come,
To a serene place where no one can,
Ever "get" to you again,
Or break your personal rules and goals,
Or rake you over the coals,
Just be nice and smile,
Knowing all the while,
If they're being mean or unruly,
To anyone or thing, acting cruelly,
That some people think too much,
Of themselves, but it's actually a crutch,
Or if they want nothing to do with you,
That's fine, because find this to be true,
That it is so very liberating,
To literally feel hostility fading.

-by Paige

Detour Poem

I took a little detour,
Got drawn by the allure,
Then I got lost,
In winding roads filled with moss,
I knew how it would go,
With being there before,
Then getting mad at myself,
I should know better I guess,
Actually, I know I should,
Just facing it, and saying it, is good,
But now where do I look?
Which way can change the road I took?
Which is the right way to go?
It's so hard, to on my own, know,
With no one telling me where to turn,
Now it's up to me to learn,
To not be so curious, or give in,
And to be more disciplined,
Not be tempted by the unknown,
It will just take me back down the wrong road,
Do I need to always get knocked?
Down or into a roadblock?
Fall and get dirty in the mud?
Or washed away by a flood?
Making myself feel sick,
Because to only myself, I did it,
I wonder how others do it,
Always stay in control and get through it,
But actually, we're all the same,
In life, trying to figure out and win this game,
Stay being, and feeling fulfilled,
Those annoying voices being stilled,
And look away without thinking,
About what I might be missing,
So I need to choose the right road,
I have, and will continue, to grow,
Because I knew how I would feel,
And I need to get off these spinning wheels,
Making the right decisions,
Not putting myself in compromising positions,
So if I sit down for awhile,
And really think deeply, I may smile,
Knowing that I do know the right way,
And it's all up to me to take it every day,
So on the road, I will get back to the fork,
And do my best to stay on course,

Because I'm stronger than I think,
And can find my way back from the brink,
Now I can get back on my path,
And again, be safe at last.

-by Paige

Chapter 5

<u>Inspirational and Uplifting</u>

Dreams Can Come True Poem

Dreams can come true,
For me, and for you,
If you stay persistent,
And never think to quit,
What you dream of,
Can become a treasure trove,
Of anything you wish,
Or desire with excited bliss,
But you have to make it real,
Don't count on others to feel,
The same passion that you do,
This is your dream to make come true,
Don't put it in others hands,
You do the work, and make the plans,
It'll even mean so much more,
Because you put in the effort for,
Every bit and piece,
Of this goal you want to reach,
So take your dreams by the reins,
And to no one do you have to explain,
Why or the reason you want it,
It's yours, and yours alone to create,
The magic you want in your life,
Your dreams, that have you enticed,
They can come true, and they will,
Just make the moves instead of staying still,
You will have them, just wait and see,
They'll be exactly, or better, than you dreamt they would be.

-by Paige

There are Good People in This World Poem

No matter all the things that come our way,
Every moment, every day,
I hope that people can realize,
And are able to see where good thrives,
It's all around us, everywhere,
But sadly, mixed with the bad, it's so unfair,
It does exist though, and it does live,
Inside of so many, with only love to give,
If something not so good happens,
It tends to take over, and dampen,
Our faith in all of humanity,
And what it is, that we believe,
But we have to have faith, and turn it around,
Think of the good, that everywhere can be found,
If we let the bad go, and turn our direction,
We just might see, in others, our own reflection,
Of good and kind, that love and nourish,
Looking down another path, we will be able to flourish,
In the ways we should, no matter what's out there,
Good or bad, away from any scare,
There are good people in this world no doubt,
More good than bad, I try to think about,
Because the world may change someday,
But it might not, so just love and pray,
But don't become jaded, and don't despair,
Know that there are people, who really genuinely care.

-by Paige

A Change of Scenery Poem

A change of scenery,
May be just what you need,
To find your true home,
So no longer you'll roam,
Where it is you can't find,
What you see in your mind,
As where you're supposed to be,
But it can be within your reach,
Never stop dreaming of it,
And never give up or quit,
Searching for your destination,
That someday you'll no longer question,
That you were meant to be there all along,
You knew deep inside you weren't wrong,
Sometimes it just takes a little change,
To make life beautifully rearrange.

-by Paige

Make Your Dreams Happen Poem

Make your dreams happen,
You have the power to,
Make them become real,
You, and only you,

In this day and age,
It's amazing by far,
How easy it is,
To become your own shining star,

Not what people think it should be,
But what you have dreamt of so far,
It doesn't matter what it is,
As long as you're happy, and feel secure,

As long as it's your dream,
And your true realism,
It doesn't matter what anyone thinks,
You hold your own wisdom,

Of what was meant for you,
To be whole, and to find yourself,
You can do it, don't stop dreaming,
Make it real, above all else,

It will mean so much to you,
If you chase it no matter what,
Anyone says or thinks,
It's your life and dreams that count.

-by Paige

Everyone's Got Something Poem

Everyone's got something,
So don't feel ashamed,
When you feel the hurt,
Or when you feel the pain,

It's actually normal,
They didn't talk about it before,
But it's finally out in the open,
With no closing of a door,

That behind it you have to hide,
To stay one way or look perfect,
No longer do we have,
To make things look so correct,

Because no one is perfect,
No matter how they make it look,
They are as imperfect as everything,
No matter how long it took,

For them to try to fake it,
And look just like the rest,
It's actually more perfect,
When you look your own true best,

Don't follow anyone,
No matter what they look like,
They are them, and you are you,
And we're all going to be alright,

No one gets out,
Without something, know that,
It's an unknown feeling,
But it's an actual fact,

We will all get through,
Know that for sure,
We're stronger than our fears,
Anything that we endure,

Be stronger than it,
Be your own self deep inside,
For you are your own strength,
For everything that you've cried,

You will be stronger than it,
And you will prevail,
Nothing will take you down,
And no one can tell your tale,

It's okay to seek help,
And it's good when you find,
Everyone is going through something,
But we can all find peace of mind,

So keep fighting it,
And don't ever let it take you down,
Because you are the only one,
That can actually turn it around.

-by Paige

Be Glad When Someone Cares Poem

Sometimes we don't see,
Exactly what people mean,
When they ask our whereabouts,
We tend to show our doubts,
At what their intentions are,
We sometimes let it mar,
Like we can't take care of ourselves,
And they're meddling, or they dwell,
On our lives, or in our business,
But sometimes it's just the opposite,
It's because they care so much,
And never want to lose touch,
And they want you to be safe,
Because to them, you can never be replaced,
See it for what it is, it's a clue,
It's the world they don't trust, not you,
They love you so much, they want to know,
Where you'll be, and everywhere you go,
So they can find you, Heaven forbid,
You do need help, or someone to lift,
You up, or back to your secure place,
Where you, and they know, you are safe,
So don't take it bad, if they're checking or knowing,
Or as if trying to be intrusive or controlling,
Know that they just care what you do,
And who, and what, is around you,
They just have concern, of you and where you are,
They care for you, whether you're near or far,
Don't ever take it for granted,
Just love that they are so enchanted,
By having you in their life,
Without you, nothing would be right,
In yours, or their world, ever again,
And regrets for not asking would deepen,
The terrible pain they would feel,
If anything were to happen, because for real,
It very unfortunately could,
But if they know where you are they would,
Always be able to help and be by your side,
They're actually a loving, caring guide,
So instead of getting upset or mad,
Be glad when someone cares enough to ask.

-by Paige

Start Fresh Poem

You can start fresh,
And feel your best,
Every day,
There's a new way,
To start again,
And make amends,
For anything yesterday,
Or standing in your way,
Of making a new life,
What to you feels right,
And move in a new direction,
With looking back, and reflection,
For what didn't work,
Or for what hurt,
You or someone else,
You can make it better yourself,
You don't always need help to,
Make changes and live up to,
Your renewed ways to live,
When you have the desire within,
Yourself, deep in your heart and soul,
When you have a mindset and goal,
You can do it yourself,
And every day, start fresh.

-by Paige

A Sparkling Jewel Poem

It's a time of renewal,
You're a sparkling jewel,
No longer a lump of coal,
You're a wonder to behold,
Poured in a new wax mold,
You've come out pure gold,
Scratches and nicks are forgotten,
No one can mistake, your newly uncommon,
Polished to shine brilliant,
Know you're worth a million,
In more than just dollars and cents,
You're captivating with your presence,
Now you know to never give up,
From a diamond in the rough,
The shine that you radiate,
Is pure beauty that you create,
You're a newly polished gem,
Precious and perfect, not pretend,
Jewelry that can't be replaced,
Your gleam is something to embrace,
You were newly poured gold,
Into a carefully carved mold,
That was broken after you were made,
Because no one can take your place,
A new you has unfolded,
Your light is purely golden,
No stone is ever the same,
Everyone is a precious gem,
Our unique colors beaming bright,
We're all such a beautiful sight,
With lovely grades of clarity,
Visible luminance a rarity,
Carat size each original,
We are all made exceptional,
Cut and color are purely perfect,
Every single one exquisite,
So always remember, you're a sparkling jewel,
We are all individually beautiful.

-by Paige

The Sea Poem

The smell of the sea,
Brings calmness to me,
The feel of the breeze,
Puts me at ease,
The rocking back and forth,
With easy gentleness, and great force,
The waters glistening,
And to nature listening,
Being sprayed with soft mists,
The taste of being salty kissed,
Whether it's overcast, or shining sunlight,
The waves crash with great might,
Waters are flowing,
Senses are easygoing,
Imagining what's underneath,
Hidden in caves and under reefs,
Another whole world of creatures live there,
Just what they're doing, we're unaware,
Playing free, loose and wild,
With the carefree spontaneity of a child,
The sea can't be tamed, ever, and shouldn't,
It's never the same, so go with the current,
How deep does it go?
We don't even know,
Dreaming of being a mermaid or sea king,
The sea opens and clears your mind, for thinking,
It's mystical and magical,
Spellbinding and fragile,
But strong, and truly magnificent,
Its beautiful colors iridescent,
Nothing else can compare,
All day and night, you could just stare,
At the lovely, twirling waves,
That completely capture your gaze,
Or just listen, with your eyes closed,
It's soothing for your soul,
The sea salt is cleansing,
While your mind is mending,
The more deeply you breathe it in,
The more you will begin,
To find a secret way to heal,
From any tension that you feel,
It calls to you, wanting you to believe,
That you too, could become a part of the sea.

-by Paige

Mesmerizing Waves and Sand Poem

Gods beauty is simply amazing,
Nothing can come close to changing,
You, to as calm as the beach and ocean can,
With their mesmerizing waves and sand,
The way it's a natural massage,
To walk in, it's a beautiful collage,
Of colors, scents and serendipity,
The serenity, you feel and see,
When the waves roll up crashing,
You can roll around in them splashing,
Giving you a natural caressing,
That's relaxing and de-stressing,
The coolness of the sea breeze blowing,
Across your warm skin, you can feel it glowing,
The entrancing, whimsical sounds,
They're everywhere, all around,
From the ocean, waves and seagulls,
Somehow, a peacefulness it fulfills,
Looking for and finding pretty shells,
All unique, in and unto themselves,
Putting one up to your ear and listening,
You can hear the sea so close, like it's whispering,
To you inside, a song coming in you deep,
Like you're part of the world underneath,
The beautiful, wild top layer,
Of the ocean, and rolling water,
If in a boat, or on the beach you stay,
It takes you away to another place,
The calling of its comfort you can't resist,
You want to stay, and never leave its salty kiss,
The beauty of a gentle, different land,
Abounds, in mesmerizing waves and sand.

-by Paige

A Gift Poem

Make your dreams come true,
Like only you can do,
It really is up to you,

Something that you love,
A gift that's yours from above,
And fits you just like a glove,

It was given to you for a reason,
You have that gift every season,
It doesn't stop, so never stop believing,

That you are able to share this gift,
And you are able to give others a lift,
When they're needing some simple bliss,

You don't need to look far to see,
It's something that comes to you naturally,
Something that you love and enjoy being,

You can become whatever you want,
What makes you happy and you always thought,
Could, and know can, become real more than not,

So whatever it is, take hold,
We are all given a talent worth more than gold,
We each have something special made from our own mold,

Know that it is yours, seen from only your eyes,
It is within your power to create, so realize,
Sharing it, will be, and is a gift from you, in other's lives.

-by Paige

Make Your Art You Poem

Whatever you do,
Make your art you,
And you will show through,

Your creative outlet,
That only you get,
Your escape at its purest,

It tells who you are,
Doing it you're a star,
The best by far,

It may be something only you understand,
Or something giving others a hand,
An art form that only you can,

Get satisfaction from,
Do with so much love,
And get so much out of,

Others may benefit as well,
If you're happy, others can tell,
Your energy is able to help,

You, and people of all ages,
Happiness is wonderfully contagious,
So own it and spread it like pages,

Of a beautiful book of love,
With your own chosen words to think of,
That show the true you, and are fun,

Whatever it is, embrace it,
Know that you never need to quit,
Because it keeps the light inside of you lit.

-by Paige

There's Beauty All Around Poem

There's beauty all around,
Everywhere it can be found,
Where there's peace and love flowing,
Like in a field of flowers growing,
Not competing with each other,
Just being with one another,
Beautiful in their own way,
Maybe even different every day,
Grass sprouting tall and green,
Brilliance shimmering clean,
Soft and wet with morning dew,
At night, a blanket of nature for you,
And for everyone to lay down or walk upon,
It flattens, but stands up again still strong,
The beautiful smells that are so bountiful,
Arouse you inside, endless joys, uncountable,
Looking up at the sky, whether it's blue or gray,
Beautiful, seeing it through the tree leaves that sway,
Wrapped in the comforting, gentle breeze,
That in itself, can put you at ease,
The sun, if it's shining, lights your way,
As the moon and stars do gloriously after the day,
Clouds may wonderfully give you shade,
As you watch them closely, at the shapes they make,
While keeping you cool, giving you a natural cover,
A safe umbrella above you, as they slowly hover,
If rain should come, or just a mist,
Feel and know, by nature you're being kissed,
Water you may find, trickling with a glimmer,
Of smooth, sweet light, from the sun, or the moons shimmer,
Everywhere you look, you can find something beautiful,
Stemming from nature, to be thankful and grateful for,
In the mountains with valleys and peaks so grand,
To the desserts with their lasting succulents and sand,
In the oceans and beaches that go as far as you can see,
To the rivers and lakes with waters of tranquility,
And if you look into the waters, you can see natures mirror,
Now look at yourself, and your beauty will become much clearer.

-by Paige

You're a Lot of Things at Heart Poem

Of a lot of things you're a part,
And you're a lot of things at heart,
Don't over analyze,
Take the time to realize,
Just how special you are,
Unique characteristics by far,
That only you have,
That are you, yourself, be glad,
Made only as you,
Real, through and through,
Don't ever give up,
No matter how rough,
The road tends to be,
Walk them freely,
For you own yourself,
You and nobody else,
No matter what you face,
Victory you will taste,
Knowing you fought the fight,
And did, for you, what's right,
Don't let people tell you what to do,
Just be honest, and show the real you,
You're more than meets the eye,
Beautiful in, and outside,
More than what shows,
Others wouldn't know,
Unless they get to really know you,
And trust me, they'd be lucky to,
See all of your love and potential,
And is so extremely essential,
To what you're made of, your being,
It's more than anyone is seeing,
It resides in your heart and soul,
You, are worth more than gold,
So in this world, never question your part,
Because you are so many beautiful things at heart.

-by Paige

Cloudy with a Chance of Sunshine Poem

It's either raining, and maybe pouring,
Or sunny, and maybe scorching,
Why can't it be perfect all the time?
Can't it just be cloudy with a chance of sunshine?
It's one way or another,
Not detouring from each other,
In any sense or form,
Trying to steer away from the storm,
Fog that won't go away,
Lift or dissipate,
Hills not seen up ahead,
Or waters that you must tread,
Danger lurks everywhere,
You have to be alert and aware,
For it can show out of nowhere,
And not even seem to care,
Who you are, it's again cloudy,
But we're all somebody,
Every living being,
We all have meaning,
So don't ever underestimate,
All your beautiful traits,
The glow you radiate,
In this world, you create.

-by Paige

Everything at Its Own Time Poem

If something's meant to be,
It will happen, you will see,
Not necessarily on your time,
Nor on my time, for mine,
But when the time is right,
That's when we can see it in our sight,
Maybe not what we asked for,
Or thought we wanted, so much more,
Than some things that we already,
Have in amounts of plenty,
We always seem to want more,
And always searching for,
The next greatest thing,
Looking to grab the brass ring,
But look at what you have,
And for all of it be glad,
Because it can be taken away in a heartbeat,
And leave you reeling in grief,
For what you're really missing,
All that time wasted guessing,
Something better was out there,
For it's time we all became aware,
Take in every single moment,
Enjoy, who to you, is the closest,
Breathe in every breath deeply,
Stay calm, and sleep sweetly,
Because fate will make it ours,
If it's supposed to be, but it's not in our power,
Or in our hands, only from above,
So what, or how much you're given, learn to love,
And just be grateful for what you have, and hold,
Onto what's yours, and keep your dreams and goals,
But if it doesn't happen, or end up to be,
What you wanted, don't cry, just believe,
It's meant to be for a reason and fate,
Accept it, and move on with grace,
For something else is meant to be,
For everyone, and differently, for you and for me,
No need to become upset or maddened,
Life will happen the way it's supposed to happen,
Because if it's meant to be, yours or mine,
It will be, but everything at its own time.

-by Paige

Things Will Work Out for the Best Poem

Things will work out for the best,
Forget about all of the rest,
They'll be the way they're supposed to be,
For you and for me,
Not what people say they should,
Or how they're supposed to look,
But actually what you push for and try,
But they only go as far as the sky,
The sky's the limit, they say,
But actually, it'll be made,
What is it meant to be for each,
Of us, and everyone, within our reach,
So don't be skeptical about anything,
Or for what life brings,
Or for what it doesn't,
Just make the best of it,
If you're early or you're late,
Maybe you missed a horrible fate,
If you did, or didn't do something,
Maybe the happiness you dreamt, it wouldn't bring,
So go with flow,
And just simply know,
Every day, night and season,
Everything happens for a reason.

-by Paige

I Love the Wind Poem

I love the wind,
When it begins,
Blowing freely,
Like it's blowing right through me,
Able to make it cool or warm,
Blowing gently, or doing harm,
You're soft, yet fierce,
You can be heard far or near,
Swaying nature beautifully,
Or tearing things down tragically,
Whatever's in your path,
You can soothe, or bring wrath,
Swaying in the trees,
With your easygoing breeze,
Or able to knock things down,
You're a force that can't be bound,
By ties or chains,
You can't be tamed,
How you make chimes sing,
Gives me a calming feeling,
You have so many sides,
Blowing with the tide,
Clearing the air,
Making debris disappear,
You amaze me with all the things that you do,
I strive to be stronger, yet gentle, like you.

-by Paige

Make It Yours Poem

When you want something,
Make it yours,
Make it happen,
Make it pure,

It'll come to you,
Maybe not today,
Maybe not tomorrow,
Don't let anything get in your way,

Because you own it,
Your own your life,
Your way and dreams,
It's not out of sight,

You can make it happen,
Your wish is your command,
Take it and own it,
It's up to you where you land,

Maybe the day after tomorrow,
Your dreams will come true,
It's all up to what you give it,
It's all up to you.

-by Paige

You're You Poem

You can be anyone you want,
But ultimately, you're you,
No matter who you are,
Or what you like to do,

You can emulate anyone,
And admire them for their qualities,
But don't let that take away,
From your own specialties,

Look at what you love,
Hold it in your grasp,
Listen to its calling,
Finally take off your mask,

Of what you've been hiding,
And of who you are,
No one can touch that,
You own it, you're a shooting star,

Above the world,
Within the light,
It's within your reach,
And in your sight,

Let nothing hold you back,
Take charge, and move forth,
For what you have to gain,
You, and everything, are worth.

-by Paige

You Were Put on This Earth for a Reason Poem

You were put on this Earth for a reason,
So never stop believing,
Know that it's a fact,
And don't ever let anyone change that,
You are special in your very own way,
Changing, yet the same, every day,
That's a good, true quality,
Everyone is able to see,
See it within yourself,
You don't need anyone else's help,
To see, feel and recognize,
The specialness, that within you lies,
No one else has your ways,
Not your voice, laugh or gaze,
The way you smile, and move,
Laugh, and walk your own groove,
Your quick or casual mind,
In only you, that someone can find,
No one has that like you,
You're irreplaceable, far and few,
Your own uniqueness,
Your facial expressions, kisses or disses,
If there's something, that of, you're not fond,
Never pretending, or being conned,
Whether you're nice and sweet,
Or straightforward without missing a beat,
It's definitely something to admire,
It's your own, unique attire,
Your wear it well and true,
And it only comes from you,
So don't ever change or waver,
From what you dislike or favor,
And you make it known, no matter what,
You own your opinions, so stand tough,
Because without you, for some, life wouldn't be worth living,
So always know, that you were put here for a reason.

-by Paige

The Wishing Well Poem

You can wish upon a star,
No matter just how far,
It is, up away from you,
And hope that it'll come true,
You can find a penny on the ground,
And believe good luck will be found,
All day long they say,
Put it in your shoe, and go on your way,
Or rub a lucky belly, who knows?
It's worth a try, the saying goes,
And if you find a four-leaf clover,
Your sorrows will be over,
Just always believe in your wishes,
Throw as many pennies in that glisten,
Beneath the water of the wishing well,
And only time will tell,
Watch it dancing, and watch it flow,
In the bottom of the water, smile and know,
That these are fun ways to find,
A peaceful, lucky state of mind,
But realize with luck and wishes,
No matter what life dishes,
The best way is to have faith,
That's where true luck is made.

-by Paige

Believe in Your Dreams Poem

Believe in yourself,
Your talent and wealth,
The love you have to give,
The life that you live,
It's yours and only yours,
No knocking down doors,
To find the real you,
The one you always knew,
And the dreams that you have,
You hold in your hand,
The ones you've wanted remain,
They're still there and are the same,
Waiting for you to take hold,
For your dreams, you're never too old,
Never stop dreaming and reaching,
For what it is that you're needing,
Craving and wanting so much,
You can have it within your clutch,
When the time is right, you will receive,
So always believe in your dreams.

-by Paige

The Sea is Endless Poem

I want to be a mermaid,
Or, a dolphin,
Either way,
I want to live in the ocean,

Where I can play all day,
Swim and just roam,
Be free and fearless,
Where I call my home,

Nothing can hurt me,
I can swiftly swim away,
From any danger,
That happens to come my way,

Where the sea is endless,
I can be anywhere,
Floating, jumping, splashing,
Without even a care,

Of what to do next,
Or things that have to get done,
It's already perfect and clean,
No chores to worry of,

The colors are all natural,
Vivid, calm and harmonious,
No other world can compare,
Under the sea, is glorious,

Dancing bubbles in the water,
Beautiful coral, reefs and caves,
That are also hideaways,
Where, if I need to, I can be safe,

But I'm safe everywhere here,
It's spacious, wild and free,
I can go anywhere I want,
Where I feel serenity, and I can just be.

-by Paige

Keep Your Chin Up Poem

Things will get better, they always do,
Even when things erupt,
There will be good and hard times,
So always keep your chin up,

Life is up and down,
Roll along with the tides,
Whatever comes your way,
Off of you, let things slide,

You can overcome anything,
Let all fears fade,
When life gives you lemons,
Like they say, make lemonade,

Lemons are good for you,
They're full of vitamins inside,
So when you're handed them,
Know that something good will arise,

Nothing good ever lasts,
That's why we should enjoy it,
The same, nothing bad ever lasts,
So don't give up or quit,

They'll both keep on coming,
Good and fun, or not so much,
But they will pass to something else,
So learn how to walk through sludge,

Because we can get through it,
And get to the other side,
So learn how to handle anything,
Life is a roller coaster ride,

No matter what you come across,
Remember, up with your chin,
We're stronger than we think,
And can handle, whatever life brings.

-by Paige

If You Don't Ask Poem

If you don't take a chance,
Or if you don't ask,
The answer will always be no,
And you'll have to let it go,
But if you do,
It's all up to you,
How it plays out,
That's what courage is about,
Out of your comfort zone,
Into the unknown,
Of what may be,
Because you can't yet see,
What lies ahead,
In dark waters you tread,
But either way you'll gain,
Whether in pride or pain,
At least a sense of knowing,
You reached out and are growing,
Nothing can hold you back,
Unless, you don't ask.

-by Paige

Nature Has No Mask Poem

Just slow down,
And listen to the sounds,
That envelope you,
When nothing's around,

They're wild and free,
They come naturally,
Nothing fake here,
Just living beings that be,

Simple as that,
Matter of fact,
Nothing will change them,
Nature will only act,

Just as it should,
And nothing else could,
Ever compare,
Come close, or ever would,

You can always trust in that,
Nature has no mask,
So when you need escape, where to?
Naturally, you don't have to ask.

-by Paige

Live Your Life Your Own Way Poem

Live your life your own way,
Who cares what other people say,
Whatever makes you happy,
Do it and be free,
Of other people's opinions,
Who cares? It doesn't diminish,
What you love to do,
It's part of what makes up you,
So never stop being yourself,
For the sake of anyone else,
To hobbies, a job or fun,
To your smile, laughter or how you run,
Whatever you do and how you do it,
Take positive, personal, proud credit,
Because it's all you, irreplaceable,
And beautiful, so don't change at all,
Always be true to who you are,
That's you, and you're unique by far.

-by Paige

Find Your Passion in Life Poem

Find your passion in life,
That is only for you and feels right,
What makes you tick,
And takes you on a trip,
Into a different place,
A moment or a space,
That is only yours to hold,
Beyond what anyone told,
You or anyone else,
Here, you can see yourself,
For who you really are,
And what you really want,
Don't ever let anyone take,
That from you, or forsake,
What you want in your life,
Because that, for you, is what's right,
You will find it one day,
Don't give up or dismay,
Whatever you like to do,
Is what's meant for you,
You'll know when you find it,
You will feel it fit,
It's been there all along,
It just takes time to find your song,
That sings it was meant for you,
That all along, deep inside, you knew,
Even if you've passed it many times,
It will come back to you sublime,
Don't ask too many questions,
Just follow your lessons,
That you're being shown,
And one day your destiny will be known.

-by Paige

Spreading Sunshine Poem

No matter if it's sunny,
Or cloudy out with rain,
Snowy or the wind blowing,
Always spread sunshine every day,

It helps you to become happy,
And deep down inside you within,
You're able to help yourself and others,
And let the smiles contagiously begin,

Gloomy weather can be dreary,
And turns smiles into a frown,
So spreading a little sunshine,
Helps turn that frown upside down,

You never know who it's going to help,
You, somebody else, everyone,
To brighten up days with sunshine,
Shining brightly, like the sun,

So whether it's warm or cold,
Or the sky is sunny or gray,
Know that spreading some sunshine,
Will brighten up everyone's day.

-by Paige

The Beauty in Quiet Poem

There's a beauty in quiet,
A gentle peace,
Calming your mind,
That can put you at ease,

It can calm your soul,
And body too,
Taking away stress,
And leave you feeling renewed,

Being able to listen,
To only natures sounds,
Can lighten your mood,
And serenity surrounds,

Enveloping you all around,
You start to feel freed,
Able to let go of worries,
Tensions released,

It's harmonious and still,
The hushed world out there,
You can catch your breath,
You become more aware,

Of "you" deep down inside,
That's been hidden and covered,
By all of life's anguish,
Slowing down, you can rediscover,

The stillness you've been needing,
And once again find your composure,
The peace of mind you've been craving,
And allow yourself to recover.

-by Paige

Take Time for Yourself Poem

Take time for yourself,
To relax and just be,
Let your mind be quiet,
No more worries,

Thoughts become clearer,
Much more positive,
Free from negativity,
No longer on the offensive,

The weight of the world,
Taken off your shoulders,
Feeling much lighter,
No more pushing boulders,

Uphill, or holding them,
Tirelessly in place,
Dodging or running from them,
Get out of the rat race,

Where you can safely stand,
And not be in harms way,
Giving you sanctity,
To begin a new day,

And keep moving forward,
With a fresh new outlook,
You can finally feel,
You're off the hook,

That aimlessly caught you,
While you were just swimming,
In the ocean of life,
And you can start a new beginning,

With a clear start ahead,
Find a sanctuary,
That's your safe place,
And danger can't be carried,

Into it, you'll be safe,
It's your own, so take a deep breath,
Nothing can take away,
The time you take for yourself.

-by Paige

I sincerely hope that you liked my poems and that they resonated, touched or helped you in some way. I love sharing them and hope you enjoyed them. Thank you so much for reading. I hope they continue to stay with you and bring inspiration and healing. As always, peace and love!

www.ingramcontent.com/pod-product-compliance
Lightning Source LLC
LaVergne TN
LVHW041321080426
835513LV00008B/539